# Leadership Teams in America's Best Schools

This book describes and demystifies the factors that have helped accomplished schools generate successful and equitable outcomes for all their students, regardless of racial/ethnic background, language, or income. Grounded in observations of award-winning schools and high-functioning teams that have achieved impressive results, this practical resource explores success from the perspective of leadership teams. As a K-12 educator at any level of leadership or within a leadership team, you can influence the success of all groups of students! This book describes *what* leadership teams do to ensure success, *why* those accomplishments are so important to the success of diverse populations of students, *why* the pursuit of those accomplishments is challenging in many schools across the country, and *how* leadership teams can take practical steps toward those accomplishments, even in difficult situations. Rich in clear examples, this book is for any educator interested in developing a deeper understanding of what their leadership teams need to change and how they might work together to lead their students to attain ambitious academic, personal, and professional goals.

**Joseph F. Johnson, Jr.**, was Founding Executive Director of the National Center for Urban School Transformation (NCUST). He is Dean Emeritus of the College of Education, and Emeritus Professor of Educational Leadership at San Diego State University, USA. He has also served as a teacher, school and district administrator, state-level administrator, and U.S. Department of Education official.

**Cynthia L. Uline** was former Director of the National Center for the 21st Century Schoolhouse. She is Professor Emeritus of Educational Leadership at San Diego State University, USA. She has also served as a teacher, teacher leader, and state-level administrator.

**Stanley J. Munro, Jr.**, is Executive Coach and Superintendent in Residence with the National Center for Urban School Transformation (NCUST) at San Diego State University. Previously, he served as a teacher, school administrator, and district administrator.

**Francisco Escobedo** is the Superintendent in Residence at the organization Leadership for Student Success. He also serves as a member of the California State Board of Education. Previously, he was the Superintendent of the Chula Vista Elementary School District, California.

# Also Available from Routledge Eye On Education
## (www.routledge.com/eyeoneducation)

**Data Analysis for Continuous School Improvement, 5th Edition**
Victoria L. Bernhardt

**Making Community Schools a Reality**
Harnessing Your Power as a School Leader through Collaboration
Emily L. Woods

**Wholehearted School Leadership**
Rewiring our Schools for Courage, Justice, Learning, and Connection
Kathryn Fishman-Weaver

**Culturally Conscious Decision-Making for School Leaders**
A Toolkit for Creating a More Equitable School Culture
Shauna McGee

**Teacher Leadership Practice in High-Performing Schools**
A Blueprint for Excellence
Jeremy D. Visone

**Coaching Education Leaders**
A Culturally Responsive Approach to Transforming Schools and Systems
Nancy B. Gutierrez, Michelle Jarney, and Michael Kim

**Teaching Practices from America's Best Urban Schools**
A Guide for School and Classroom Leaders, 2nd Edition
Joseph F. Johnson, Cynthia L. Uline, and Lynne G. Perez

**Leadership in America's Best Urban Schools**
Joseph F. Johnson, Cynthia L. Uline, and Lynne G. Perez

**When Black Students Excel**
How Schools Can Engage and Empower Black Students
Joseph F. Johnson, Jr., Cynthia L. Uline, and Stanley J. Munro, Jr.

**Five Practices for Improving the Success of Latino Students**
A Guide for Secondary School Leaders
Christina Theokas, Mary L. Gonzalez, Consuela Manriquez, and Joseph F. Johnson

**Fostering Parent Engagement for Equitable and Successful Schools**
A Leader's Guide to Supporting Families and Students
Patrick Darfler-Sweeny

**Empowering Teacher Leadership**
Strategies and Systems to Realize Your School's Potential
Jeremy D. Visone

# Leadership Teams in America's Best Schools

Improving the Lives of All Students

Joseph F. Johnson, Jr.,
Cynthia L. Uline, Stanley J. Munro, Jr.,
and Francisco Escobedo

NEW YORK AND LONDON

Designed cover image: © Getty Images

First published 2026
by Routledge
605 Third Avenue, New York, NY 10158

and by Routledge
4 Park Square, Milton Park, Abingdon, Oxon, OX14 4RN

*Routledge is an imprint of the Taylor & Francis Group, an informa business*

© 2026 Joseph F. Johnson, Jr., Cynthia L. Uline, Stanley J. Munro, Jr., and Francisco Escobedo

The right of Joseph F. Johnson, Jr., Cynthia L. Uline, Stanley J. Munro, Jr., and Francisco Escobedo to be identified as authors of this work has been asserted in accordance with sections 77 and 78 of the Copyright, Designs and Patents Act 1988.

All rights reserved. No part of this book may be reprinted or reproduced or utilised in any form or by any electronic, mechanical, or other means, now known or hereafter invented, including photocopying and recording, or in any information storage or retrieval system, without permission in writing from the publishers.

*Trademark notice*: Product or corporate names may be trademarks or registered trademarks, and are used only for identification and explanation without intent to infringe.

ISBN: 978-1-032-93510-2 (hbk)
ISBN: 978-1-032-93509-6 (pbk)
ISBN: 978-1-003-56623-6 (ebk)

DOI: 10.4324/9781003566236

Typeset in Optima
by Apex CoVantage, LLC

This book is dedicated to the memory of
our inspiring friend and dedicated colleague
Cara Riggs

# Contents

| | | |
|---|---|---|
| | *List of NCUST Award-Winning School Vignettes* | viii |
| | *Meet the Authors* | x |
| | *Preface* | xiii |
| | *Acknowledgments* | xxiii |
| 1 | Overview: The Gears That Drive Success for All Students | 1 |
| 2 | Effective Leadership Teams | 26 |
| 3 | Positive Transformational Culture | 51 |
| 4 | Rigorous Curricula | 75 |
| 5 | Effective Initial Instruction | 98 |
| 6 | Monitoring, Confirming, and Enhancing Learning | 122 |
| 7 | Effective Intervention and Enrichment | 150 |
| 8 | The Role of District Leaders | 172 |
| | Conclusion | 195 |

 # NCUST Award-Winning School Vignettes

**Vignette A:** Horace Mann Elementary School, Glendale Unified School District, Glendale, California

**Vignette B:** Paul Laurence Dunbar Young Men's Leadership Academy, Fort Worth Independent School District, Fort Worth, Texas

**Vignette C:** Veterans Memorial Early College High School, Brownsville Independent School District, Brownsville, Texas

**Vignette D:** P.S. 249, The Caton School, New York City Department of Education, District 14, Brooklyn, New York

**Vignette E:** Dr. Americo Parades Elementary School, Brownsville Independent School District, Brownsville, Texas

**Vignette F:** Richard Gahr High School, ABC Unified School District, Cerritos, California

**Vignette G:** Wynnebrook Elementary, Palm Beach County School District, West Palm Beach, Florida

**Vignette H:** Stillman Middle School, Brownsville Independent School District, Brownsville, Texas

**Vignette I:** P.S. 171, Patrick Henry Preparatory School, New York City Department of Education, District 4, East Harlem, New York

**Vignette J:** Silver Wing Elementary School, Chula Vista Elementary School District, Chula Vista, California

**Vignette K:** Feaster Charter School, Chula Vista Elementary School District, Chula Vista, California

**Vignette L:** R. F. Hazard Elementary, Garden Grove Unified School District, Garden Grove, California

**Vignette M:** Benavides Elementary, Brownsville Independent School District, Brownsville, Texas

**Vignette N:** P.S. 359, Leaders of Excellence, Advocacy, and Discovery (LEAD), Bronx, New York

**Vignette O:** Brownsville Independent School District, Brownsville, Texas

# Meet the Authors

**Joseph F. Johnson, Jr.**, is the Founding Executive Director of the National Center for Urban School Transformation at San Diego State University. He has served as a teacher, school administrator, district administrator, and state-level administrator in Texas and Ohio and as the Director of the federal Title I program for the U.S. Department of Education. In higher education, Dr. Johnson has served as a professor of educational leadership, as dean of the college of education, and as interim provost and senior vice president at San Diego State University. His research focuses upon schools that achieve remarkable academic results for diverse populations of students. He is also an author of *When Black Students Excel, Teaching Practices in America's Best Urban Schools, Leadership in America's Best Urban Schools,* and *Five Practices for Improving the Success of Latino Students: A Practical Guide for Secondary School Leaders.*

**Cynthia L. Uline** is Professor Emeritus of Educational Leadership at San Diego State University. Cynthia served as Director of SDSU's National Center for the 21st Century Schoolhouse and Director of SDSU's Doctoral Program in Educational Leadership. She has also served as a teacher, teacher leader, and state education agency administrator. Cynthia's research explores the influence of built learning environments on students' learning, as well as the roles leaders, teachers, students, and the public play in shaping learning spaces. Her current research considers the potential of green schools as student-centered, ecologically responsive, and economically viable places for learning. She has also published journal articles, books, and book chapters related to leadership for learning, leadership preparation, and schools that achieve remarkable academic results for diverse populations of students. Her latest books include *A Practical Guide for Leading Green Schools: Partnering with Nature to Create Vibrant, Flourishing Sustainable Schools*, co-authored with Lisa A.W. Kensler, and *When Black Students Excel*.

**Stanley J. Munro, Jr.**, is an Executive Coach with the National Center for Urban School Transformation (NCUST) at San Diego State University, where he has promoted the best practices of high-performing urban schools and districts throughout the nation. Throughout his 24-year professional career in education, he has faithfully served as a teacher, curriculum writer, job-embedded professional developer, assistant principal, principal, executive director, assistant superintendent, and superintendent. Dr. Munro received a bachelor of science from the University of Toronto; a master's degree from Harvard University in management; master's degrees in school administration and supervision, teaching mathematics, and as a reading specialist from Johns Hopkins University; and a doctor of education in educational leadership from San Diego State University. During his career, Dr. Munro's most important work has been that of a student advocate. His mission, vision, values, and goals are firmly rooted in the fact that as educators, the unwavering responsibility is to prepare each scholar for jobs that have not been created with technology that has not been invented, to solve problems that don't exist currently. Dr. Stanley J. Munro is married to his wife Mrs. Yovana Munro, who is a licensed marriage and family therapist. Together, they have two children.

**Francisco Escobedo** is the Superintendent in Residence for Leadership for Student Success, an organization dedicated to empowering superintendents as transformative leaders capable of reshaping school systems. He also serves on California's State Board of Education and the Board of Directors for WestEd. Previously, Dr. Escobedo was Executive Director of the National Center for Urban School Transformation and has dedicated over 33 years to education. From 2010 to 2021, he served as Superintendent of the Chula Vista Elementary School District (CVESD), overseeing 46 schools and more than 29,400 students. Under his leadership, CVESD was recognized as a "California Positive Outlier" district by the Learning Policy Institute in 2019. The district also received awards such as the California Association for Bilingual Education's Multiple Pathways to Biliteracy

## Meet the Authors

District Award for its 22 dual immersion schools and the California Department of Education's Exemplary District of the Year Award in 2018. Since 2001, Dr. Escobedo has been an adjunct professor of Educational Leadership at San Diego State University (SDSU), where he also serves on the doctoral faculty. He holds a BA from Yale University; an MA from SDSU; and an EdD from the University of California, San Diego, and SDSU.

# Preface

We wrote this book because we hope to see many more schools become places where all groups of students succeed academically and socially. We have found, visited, and admired schools across this nation where students of all races/ethnicities, family income levels, and language backgrounds accurately perceive they are becoming capable scholars who can think independently, solve problems logically, and interact with others respectfully. We are convinced that many more schools can achieve similar results.

We listened to enthusiastic second-grade students in East Harlem as they worked in small groups to organize and present detailed reports on the physical characteristics and the biological needs of a praying mantis. As the students eagerly engaged in developing and sharing their written and oral reports, their faces sparkled with pride as they accurately utilized scientific terms other children don't learn until middle school or high school.

We watched in awe as sixth graders, living in low-income neighborhoods just a few miles north of Tijuana, Mexico, participated in Socratic seminars, engaging each other in detailed discussions about the author's intent and the author's use of literary devices, as they developed their understanding of a novel. As they utilized both their native language and their rapidly growing command of English, the students, many of whom were considered "English learners" only a few years before, knew they were reading, understanding, and discussing complex English texts appropriate for students at or beyond their grade level.

In a secondary school in Fort Worth, Texas, we observed Black/African American and Latino/Hispanic middle school students who explained real-world algebraic problems accurately, detailed the steps needed to solve the problem, explained why the steps were logical, and provided strategies for determining the accuracy of their answers. The students were not a select group chosen for their perceived capacity to learn algebra. In contrast, the students were typical children who were being taught in a way that was helping them believe they all could master algebraic concepts.

We observed students of various racial/ethnic backgrounds in a high school just outside of St. Louis, Missouri, as they constructed and described three-dimensional models that illustrated how insulin helps a healthy body move glucose from the blood stream into cells where it can be stored as energy. Then, the students modified their models to show what happens when insulin is insufficient (as happens with Type I diabetes) or when the body does not respond appropriately to insulin (as happens with Type 2 diabetes). As many of the students explained their models, they talked about the impact of diabetes on their family members and friends. The students were learning they could understand and communicate about important physiological functions that influenced the lives of people around them.

We read articulate summaries, essays, reports, and poetry written by students who might have struggled to write a sentence only a few years prior. We observed classes in which all students (including students with disabilities) presented and explained detailed projects that modeled their accurate understanding of complex ideas. We saw groups of students working together in a civil, respectful manner to resolve interpersonal conflicts or to evaluate potential solutions to complex local issues that shape the quality of life experienced by their families and neighbors. We watched students of all ages demonstrate respect for themselves and for others from different races, ethnicities, language backgrounds, religions, physical or intellectual abilities, socio-economic backgrounds, genders, and sexual identities. We have seen and studied schools where these and similar successes are common, where students are proud of their academic accomplishments and enthusiastic about their prospects for future success in school and in life. While all these schools acknowledge room for improvement and all of them work tirelessly to maintain outstanding outcomes for all demographic groups, these amazing schools lead us to believe that so many more schools can become places where all demographic groups of students achieve academic proficiency, evidence a love of learning, and graduate well prepared to succeed in post-secondary education, the workplace, and their communities. We wrote this book with the hope of helping more schools emulate the systems and adapt the practices that can generate greater outcomes, especially for groups of students who have historically been underserved.

## More Than Test Scores

We wrote this book because we know that students need, parents demand, and communities expect more than good test scores. As well, we wrote this book because we believe some schools have pursued better test scores in ways that do little to increase students' understanding of important concepts or in ways that might decrease the extent to which students experience the joy of learning. This book is based upon schools that generate abundant evidence that all demographic groups of students can learn to love learning and master challenging academic standards while simultaneously performing well on standards-based assessments.

Since 2006, the National Center for Urban School Transformation has been identifying outstanding schools in a wide array of communities where all demographic groups of students enjoy impressive academic successes. Their students graduate well prepared to succeed in post-secondary education, the workplace, and their communities. These schools also generate outstanding results on state assessments. In fact, each of the schools boasts test scores that exceed the averages for all students in their respective states. Additionally, each of the schools boasts test scores for each racial/ethnic and income group that exceed the averages for all students in the state. To view the current criteria NCUST uses to select America's Best Schools, please see https://ncust.com/americas-best-urban-schools-award-eligibility-criteria/.

For example, in the 2022–2023 school year, students who met low-income criteria at Horace Mann Elementary in the Glendale Unified School District in Glendale, California, were more likely to demonstrate proficiency on state assessments in mathematics than all elementary students throughout California. Similarly, in 2022–2023, Latino students at Veterans Memorial High School in Brownsville, Texas, were more likely to demonstrate proficiency on state assessments in English than all high school students in Texas. As well, both Black and Latino students at Gahr High School in Cerritos, California (in Los Angeles County), were more likely to demonstrate proficiency on state assessments in both English language arts and mathematics than high school students throughout California.

It is important to note, however, that state assessment results were only one indicator of the success of these schools. Schools were required to submit attendance data, student discipline data (including suspension and expulsion data disaggregated by student groups), data regarding the progress of students who are emerging as multi-lingual learners, data regarding the progress of students with disabilities, and graduation data (disaggregated by student groups). NCUST endeavored to ensure that each finalist for the "America's Best School" Award was leading all demographic groups of students to experience academic growth and success in ways that would positively affect their lives.

Each finalist school received intensive on-site visits during which visit teams observed classrooms and teacher collaboration meetings; interviewed students, parents, teachers, and administrators; and examined a variety of data sources. Site visit teams saw students who might have been underserved and uninspired if they attended more typical schools in the same town or city. Yet, in the finalist schools, the teams observed many examples of students excelling, growing, and developing a love of learning. Frequently, students told the site visit team members about their academic accomplishments, their goals, and their plans to continue their education. Often teachers explained that state standards defined "the floor" of knowledge and skill they aimed to lead all their students to master, while "the ceiling" was defined only by the aspirations and dreams of their students. Often parents expressed pride in the concepts and skills their children were learning successfully. Many parents believed their children would have opportunities to make a positive difference in their lives and in the lives of their communities.

Even though test scores were impressive, they often were overshadowed by the rigor of classroom conversations, the complexity of student projects, or the quality of student written or oral presentations. Students from all races, ethnicities, language backgrounds, genders, and family income levels demonstrated they were capable readers, thoughtful problem solvers, imaginative mathematicians, proficient writers, and analytical scientists. At the same time, many of the same students had learned to enjoy and appreciate art, music, drama, physical education, and similar pursuits, often in ways that built upon their knowledge of core academic content. Students exuded a sense of efficacy that they could succeed academically, learn challenging concepts and skills, and use what they learned to improve their lives and the lives of others.

We call these schools "America's Best Schools" not because they have the best scores on state assessments or any other metric. They are our best schools because they positively influence the lives of every demographic group they serve. We wrote this book in support of dedicated educators who want to ensure that all their students, regardless of race, ethnicity, family income level, language background, or any other demographic characteristic, experience learning environments that prepare them to pursue their dreams and make a difference in their lives and in the lives of their communities.

## The Power of Leadership Teams

Many authors have written about the importance of great teachers who enhance the academic success of their students. As well, other writers have chronicled the impact of principals and other school leaders who play critical roles in improving learning results. We wrote this book, however, because we hope to deepen understanding of the power of leadership teams (administrative leaders, teacher leaders, parent leaders, community leaders, and student leaders) who work together in ways that make learning more likely for all groups of students.

While teachers, school administrators, and district leaders play huge roles in shaping improvements, they are much more likely to be successful when they listen carefully to the voices of students, solicit sincerely the input of parents, and work honestly with community leaders to articulate concerns and acquire support for courses of action that can lead to improvements in learning results.

Among all the amazing schools we have studied, we have not found even one where a leader (regardless of position, power, or title) was able to initiate, organize, implement, and sustain a successful improvement effort without the active support of an array of committed team members. Similarly, even though we have visited hundreds of schools with talented, dedicated team members in a variety of positions, we cannot point to even one that accomplished and sustained substantial improvements in learning outcomes without the constructive engagement of at least one administrative leader.

In America's best schools, we find teams working together to identify strengths, learn more about underlying needs, challenge prevailing assumptions, refine approaches, and celebrate growth. High-functioning teams are the engines that transform quarts of effort into barrels of learning. High-functioning teams use everyone's insights, wisdom, experience, and skills in ways that help people know they are valued members of a professional community. In high-functioning teams, team members are always learning (even though people rarely feel criticized for what they don't know) and always contributing to the learning of others. High-functioning teams are generally not surprised when their students achieve outstanding academic results. They believe in their students. They believe in their colleagues. They believe in their collective work. We wrote this book to make clear how your teams can work together and achieve substantial learning improvements for all the groups of students you serve.

## Intended Audience

This book is intended for educators who believe in the potential of every student, regardless of their demographic background, to achieve at high levels. If you're unsure whether all student groups in your classroom, school, or district can succeed, we encourage you to explore examples of similar schools where all students are thriving. Witnessing their success may inspire new perspectives and approaches to supporting every learner. We are confident that when you have seen schools similar to those that informed and inspired this book, you will be eager to engage your colleagues in reading these pages and collectively determining how you can generate similar learning outcomes for the students and families you serve.

We acknowledge there may be many bureaucratic, financial, political, racial, or administrative challenges impeding the success of your classroom, school, or district. In all our many visits to amazing schools, we have not heard teacher leaders, school leaders, or district leaders claim their successes were achieved quickly or easily. We know every school faces real and exhausting challenges; however, we wrote this book for teams of educators who are willing to assume they can still make a powerful difference, even an amazing difference, especially for students who historically have not been served well. Effective leadership teams begin with team members (regardless of job title) who are willing to listen to others' perspectives, learn about other approaches, reflect, grow, and improve, as they model personal accountability, as well as sincere respect for all their team members.

If you are expecting to find within these pages miraculous, earth-shattering ideas and quick remedies to "fix" children, parents, teachers, or administrators, you will probably be disappointed. Instead, we have learned that systems need to be "fixed" so every child served feels loved and challenged; every parent feels heard and respected; every educator feels guided and supported to ensure every child's success; and every administrator is committed to supporting every student, parent, and educator in ways that make success likely. The truth is everything we have learned from America's Best Schools has been identified, studied, and described by educational leaders such as Karen Chenowith, Linda Darling-Hammond, Lisa Delpit, Rick and Becky Dufour, Ron Edmonds, Ron Ferguson, Doug Fisher, Nancy Frey, Michael Fullan, Patricia Gándara, Geneva Gay, Zaretta Hammond, Frank Harris, John Hattie, Katie Haycock, Tyrone Howard, Gloria Ladson-Billings, Larry Lezotte, Kenneth Leithwood, Gholdy Muhammad, Robert Marzano, Anthony Muhammad, Sonia Nieto, Pedro Noguera, Jeannie Oakes, Glenn Singleton, Megan Tschannen-Moran, Grant Wiggins, and Luke Wood. This book shares how leadership teams took many important ideas and pieced them together logically and coherently, often one step at a time, in a systemic way that worked to make measurable, profound differences for their students.

We wrote this book for teams of educators who know they can help their students achieve more. We wrote this for leadership teams who believe they can work together to make a difference that can change the trajectory of their students' lives. This book is for leadership teams who recognize that achieving substantially better outcomes is likely to require making some important changes. At the same time, however, we wrote this book for teams who can accept that the 174 schools that have earned NCUST's America's Best School Award (as of 2024) have made these important changes with mortal teachers, with fallible leaders, in imperfect school districts, usually amid a myriad of other frustrations and distractions. (The full list of NCUST award-winning schools is available at https://ncust.com/previous-americas-best-urban-schools-award-winners/.) If you believe it can be done in your classroom, your school, or your district, we wrote this book for you. We want to show you clearly what leadership teams sought to change within their schools and districts, we want you to understand why those changes are important, and we want to help you understand why it is often difficult to make those changes. Finally, we want to provide an abundance of clear, powerful examples of how real schools pursued and achieved those difficult changes in ways that ultimately led to wonderful outcomes for the various groups of students they serve.

## How This Book Can Help

Even though all 174 schools NCUST has awarded are different, there are important commonalities that influenced better learning outcomes for all the student groups served in each school. Chapter 1 will provide an overview of the commonalities by introducing the metaphor of a set of gears that work together to drive change in ways that substantially improve outcomes for all student groups. In clear language, with practical examples, we will explain how these six gears have worked in the schools NCUST has identified, awarded, and studied over the past two decades. Through this overview, your leadership team will begin to see a complete picture of what may be working and what may not be working to generate outstanding learning results for your students. Each of the six gears can play a role in accelerating progress toward your goals for your students. However, Chapter 1 will also clarify how progress can be hampered or stalled if the gears do not connect with each other or if one or more gear gets stuck.

Chapter 1 (like all eight chapters) will begin with vignettes that describe two schools that won NCUST's America's Best Schools Award. In Chapter 1, these stories will help illustrate how the six gears worked together to create impressive student successes. The vignettes will provide practical examples of what school teams sought to accomplish as they worked to move all six gears in ways that maximized the success of all student groups.

Starting in Chapter 1, as in many of our previous books, we will include a "What It Is/What It Isn't" feature that helps differentiate successful schools from schools where positive efforts can be found yet improvements in outcomes are not forthcoming. Also, starting in Chapter 1, this book will introduce a new feature: "Tips for Leadership Teams." This list of practical suggestions is not a traditional checklist of "one and done" items because the most important things are never "done." Instead, we encourage leadership teams to review the "Tips for Teams" on at least a monthly basis to remind them to keep focused on the issues that are most likely to influence their success.

Chapters 2 through 7 will each highlight one the six gears described in Chapter 1. As in Chapter 1, each of the following chapters will include two vignettes from outstanding schools that NCUST has awarded; however, these vignettes will focus on the specific gear highlighted in the chapter. Using the vignettes as examples, each chapter will specifically address **what** leadership teams should strive to create/build in order to ensure that the gear is functioning optimally and will lead your school to better outcomes for all student groups, **why** many leadership teams have difficulty optimizing the gear, and **how** leadership teams can ensure that the gear moves in a way that advances the success of all student groups. Chapters 2 through 7 will also include a rubric that can guide school leadership teams in assessing their progress in advancing the gear discussed within the chapter.

While the first seven chapters will focus primarily on the role of school leadership teams, Chapter 8 will specifically address how district leadership teams can influence the success of school leadership teams. We recognize that schools are much more likely to change in ways that improve students' lives if district leaders work in ways that support school leadership teams well.

In Chapter 8, we suggest how district leaders can create a district-level context that helps all their schools best attend to the issues described in Chapters 1 through 7. We provide specific suggestions about how district leadership teams can maximize focus and coherence while minimizing distractions that decrease the capacity of schools to generate great outcomes for all groups of students. Similar to the preceding chapters, Chapter 8 will include a "What It Is/What It Isn't" section that clarifies the kinds of district-level action that may be needed to support school leadership teams. As well, Chapter 8 will offer a "Tips for District Leaders" that specifies recommendations to district leadership teams for their ongoing attention in support of schools.

We feel privileged to have learned from so many of America's best schools. With this privilege, we feel tremendous responsibility to elevate the most critical issues, accurately describe the most perplexing challenges, and reinforce the most powerful lessons learned by leadership teams that have advanced the academic success of all their students. We wrote this book because we want to see your school meet NCUST's America's Best School award criteria. We know that for every school NCUST has awarded, there are a hundred more with the potential to positively change the trajectory of the lives of the students they serve. We wrote this book to support your success as you endeavor to support the success of your students.

# Acknowledgments

This book represents our sincere effort to share what we have learned from exemplary leaders and educators in schools and school districts that generate outstanding learning results for all student groups, including demographic groups who, historically, have been underserved. We are deeply grateful to educators who have opened their districts, schools, and classrooms, allowing us to learn how they have achieved successes that have eluded our nation in general. We feel privileged to have enjoyed opportunities to observe classroom learning activities, watch teachers working together to plan stimulating lessons, hear team leaders engage their colleagues in discussions of student work, hear principals describe how they dealt with setbacks and frustrations, listen to parents describe the outreach they have experienced from teachers, and hear students (of all ages, races, language backgrounds, and family incomes) tell us why they love coming to school and learning. Without their input, we would have no output to offer. This book exists only because of their exceptional successes and their willingness to share the stories behind their successes with us. Over the past 20 years, NCUST has awarded over 170 schools. While this book mentions (directly or indirectly) many of the awardees, this book includes 14 vignettes about specific award-winning schools. As well, we have included a vignette about one school district that is the home of 13 NCUST award-winning schools.

We also acknowledge the thousands of educators around the nation who are eager to improve educational outcomes for the students they serve. Their sincere commitment to pursuing learning outcomes similar to those achieved by NCUST award-winning schools is a tremendous inspiration. This book is designed especially for teams of educators as they consider

## Acknowledgments

how they might work together to lead their students to attain ambitious academic, personal, and professional goals.

This book did not begin with us. Our work builds upon a tradition of scholarship and inquiry started by heroic educators such as Ron Edmonds and Larry Lezotte and extended through the work of others such as Karin Chenoweth, Lisa Delpit, Ron Ferguson, Doug Fisher, Nancy Frey, Geneva Gay, Zaretta Hammond, John Hattie, Kati Haycock, Tyrone Howard, Gloria Ladson-Billings, Ellen Moir, Anthony Muhammad, Gholdy Muhammad, Pedro Noguera, Jeannie Oaks, Doug Reeves, James Scheurich, and Linda Skrla. These leaders insisted that our nation's children deserved schools that generated excellent learning outcomes for every student group, including those groups who, historically, have not been served well.

We especially acknowledge the strong support of our colleagues at San Diego State University and the National Center for Urban School Transformation. A former SDSU president, Stephen Weber, and a former dean of SDSU's College of Education, Lionel "Skip" Meno, envisioned a national center that would identify, study, and promote excellence and equity in urban schools. They secured initial funding support from the Qualcomm Corporation, and they creatively provided other support that helped us start the National Center for Urban School Transformation (NCUST). The current SDSU president, Adela De la Torre; the current SDSU College of Education dean, Y. Barry Chung; the chair of the Department of Educational Leadership, Douglas Fisher; and the new NCUST executive director, Greg Ottinger, continue to provide remarkable support for our efforts. San Diego State University has been a great home for NCUST, in part because of the outstanding faculty, staff, and students who have been important collaborators in our efforts.

Finally, we acknowledge the time, wisdom, and commitment of our colleagues and staff at NCUST. We are honored to work with and learn from a team of executive coaches who have experience leading and/or supporting high-performing schools. NCUST was initiated and shaped through the work of former executive coaches, superintendents-in-residence, and leaders Barbra Balser, Tony Burks, Debbie Costa-Hernandez, Gina Gianzero, Jose Iniguez, Karen Janney, Lynne Perez, Cara Riggs, Hazel Rojas, and Christina Theokas. Today, the Center flourishes through the work of current executive coaches and superintendents-in-residence Angela Bass, Rupi Boyd, Tavga Bustani, Vincent Matthews, Debra McLaren, Shirley Peterson,

Sid Salazar, Matthew Tessier, Jeff Thiel, Luz Vicario, and Granger Ward. Also, our work has been supported superbly by Jocelyn Falco, Karen Jones, and Mark Wilson. These talented individuals have committed themselves to identifying, studying, and promoting the best practices of America's best schools. This book would not exist without their efforts.

# 1 | Overview
## The Gears That Drive Success for All Students

> **Voices of Students and Parents From America's Best Schools**
>
> "At Horace Mann we learn hard things because everybody makes learning easy for us. . . . Well, not really easy, but they make it seem easy when we work hard."
>
> > – Miguel, fourth-grade student,
> > Horace Mann Elementary, Glendale, CA
>
> "My parents were educators who made sure I attended private schools or charter schools throughout my elementary years, so I had been accustomed to being one of the few Black students in my school. In 2012, when YMLA first opened, I started as a seventh-grade student. It was my first experience in a school where 60% of the students were African American, 40% were Mexican American, and all the students were boys. I really had to adjust. At YMLA, we were constantly hearing and speaking positive messages about ourselves. We had a creed and a mission. We were always reciting them and building ourselves up. Every morning, we were using positive language that helped us see ourselves as scholars and productive citizens. The powerful verbal messages were reinforced by even more powerful relationships. We didn't just go to school with other students. We were a family. The teachers knew us. They knew our families. I knew the principal and he knew my name. The teachers acted like they had a vested interest in us. And then, there was this hyper focus on academic success. Our teachers wanted us to succeed academically, but they also wanted us

to succeed in life. So, they really wanted us to understand the material. Now that I have graduated, I'm a student at Texas Christian University. I look forward to becoming a teacher and making a difference for students the way that YMLA made a difference for me."

– Taylor, 2018 graduate of Young Men's Leadership Academy, Fort Worth, TX

"The dream team is what we call our teachers here, because they make our dreams come true. They work hard so we can accomplish our dreams. I think Mr. White [the principal] came up with that name. The teachers go above and beyond to make sure we can achieve our dreams."

– Ezra, 11th-grade student, Young Men's Leadership Academy, Fort Worth, TX

"The teachers at Horace Mann are on a mission to help you learn and succeed. They think we are smart, so they push us to be smart. They think we can learn anything, so they help make sure we learn everything we need to learn."

– Arkina, fifth-grade student, Horace Mann Elementary, Glendale, CA

## VIGNETTE A: Horace Mann Elementary School, Glendale Unified School District, Glendale, California

**WON NCUST'S AMERICA'S BEST SCHOOL AWARD IN 2010, 2016, 2020, AND 2024**

*When Rosa Alonso became principal of Horace Mann Elementary, the school was considered the lowest-achieving school in Glendale, California. Most of the school's students were not experiencing academic success. Principal Alonso explained, "Rigor varied from teacher to teacher, even within the same grade level. There was inconsistency in curriculum and in instructional practices. Lesson delivery was erratic. We seemed to be working more as independent contractors than as grade-level or school teams."*

In the following years, although the student population remained similar, learning results improved and the school earned many accolades. In 2018 and 2020, the California Department of Education recognized Horace Mann as a California Distinguished School. In 2010, 2016, 2020, and 2024, NCUST awarded Horace Mann the America's Best School Award. As well, in 2023, the U.S. Department of Education designated Horace Mann Elementary as a National Blue Ribbon School.

What changed? How did the lowest-performing school in the city of Glendale, California, become one of the highest performing in the nation? Why is it that state assessment results, samples of student work, parent interviews, and classroom observations suggest that all student groups at Horace Mann are achieving levels of success that will positively influence their lives in middle school, high school, and beyond?

Principal Alonso explained that initially teams of teachers came together to prioritize what they wanted their students to accomplish. She said, "We asked, what are the highest-priority standards? What does proficiency look like at each grade level? We wanted teachers to have a common understanding of what students needed to learn."

Then, she explained, "By identifying the most critical standards, we were able to spend time carefully analyzing the standards and developing common assessments to measure students' progress in mastering those standards." Common assessments became a school-wide tool for ensuring that every student was making progress toward mastering the most important challenging academic skills.

To maximize student success with the new common assessments, Horace Mann leaders structured opportunities for teachers to work together to improve day-to-day instruction. Each week, teachers had time to meet in grade-level teams "to design lessons based on the focus standards and identify lesson objectives." Principal Alonso explained that the collaboration meetings allowed teachers time to ask themselves, "How do we break down the thinking process so students understand [challenging concepts]?" She elaborated, "During these collaboration meetings, teachers also look at student work and analyze students' performance on the grade-level developed assessment. They discuss . . . what were areas of difficulty and what are next steps to improve students' understanding. They identify which students got it and which students need more support, but more importantly, they feel empowered to make the right things happen . . . one step at a time."

Many teachers and paraprofessionals told the NCUST reviewers that school leaders wanted them to succeed. Teachers expressed pride about being part of a team that was helping all groups of students succeed. Parents expressed awe at the many ways Horace Mann educators demonstrated that they cared for, and believed in, their children. Students were eager to attempt challenging tasks and persist through difficult assignments, because they believed they were as bright and capable as their teachers told them they were.

## VIGNETTE B: Paul Laurence Dunbar Young Men's Leadership Academy, Fort Worth Independent School District, Fort Worth, Texas

**WON NCUST'S AMERICA'S BEST SCHOOL AWARD IN 2015 AND 2018**

In 2012, Rodney White became the first principal of Young Men's Leadership Academy (YMLA), a public school serving exclusively male students in the Fort Worth Independent School District. When the first series of district interim assessments placed YMLA near the bottom of the district's 30 middle schools, Principal White shared the data with students and with the YMLA staff. He helped everyone understand how the data might lead others to think about YMLA's predominantly Black and Brown student population. He challenged teachers to develop and implement plans that would move YMLA toward becoming one of the district's top five middle schools. Similarly, he challenged students to establish individual and group goals that would change the city's perception of YMLA.

During the ensuing months and years, YMLA educators and students focused upon establishing a culture in which students felt a deep sense of belonging, connection, and brotherhood. Students came to see themselves as responsible for working hard to ensure their individual academic progress, as well as contributing to the progress of their brother schoolmates. Teachers committed to recognizing and celebrating individual and group efforts that promoted leadership, positive behavior, and academic progress.

Teachers worked together to ensure they were teaching students the challenging standards that were the focus of district assessments, as well as state assessments in English, mathematics, science, and social studies. To ensure that lessons were designed to ensure students learned specific critical standards, school leaders conducted regular observations and provided consistent feedback that focused on the alignment between the lesson's objective and the academic standards students needed to master.

Similarly, teachers helped students focus on what they needed to learn by helping students establish specific goals and develop action plans for achieving those goals and monitoring their implementation of their action plans. Students began to see real progress as they pursued ambitious academic goals. Students began to see themselves as capable scholars.

Improved learning results did not appear automatically. Teachers and administrators shifted away from a focus on the district's scope and sequence charts and instead focused more on giving students sufficient time to develop deep understanding of the most important concepts and skills. As well, teachers focused more on designing lessons that would actively engage their students in "doing, creating, and discussing" rather than "just sitting and listening."

Students at YMLA refer to their teachers as "the dream team" because "they make our dreams come true." YMLA has earned recognition from the Texas Education Agency, GreatSchools.com, and Common Sense, as well as NCUST, for their successes in leading high percentages of students to graduate well prepared to succeed in post-secondary education.

## Why Learning Outcomes Vary Among Similar Schools

When our National Center for Urban School Transformation teams visit finalists for our America's Best School Award, we are often intrigued to see educators using some of the same curricular programs we find when we visit schools where many student groups are not enjoying academic success. Conversely, in struggling schools, we will usually find at least a few classrooms where teachers model the same outstanding teaching practices we find in our award-winning schools. Often, in both the highest-performing schools and the schools struggling through great frustrations, we hear teachers describe a similar focus on state standards, we find passionate principals who strive to promote better learning outcomes, and we find educators who work tirelessly to improve teaching and learning. Nonetheless, the overall differences are profound.

The learning results achieved at NCUST award-winning schools cannot be predicted by student characteristics (such as race, ethnicity, or prior school success) or family characteristics (such as family income or home language), because students in our award-winning schools achieve at remarkable levels, regardless of how they might be labeled, categorized, or grouped. Outstanding learning results are predictable and logical because leadership teams have built, and set in motion, systems that work to continuously improve teaching and learning for all students.

For two decades, NCUST has been studying schools that achieve outstanding learning results for all groups of students. Horace Mann Elementary in Glendale, California (described in Vignette A), and Young Men's Leadership Academy in Fort Worth, Texas (described in Vignette B), are 2 of the more than 170 schools NCUST has identified, awarded, and studied. We have sought to understand what these impressive schools accomplish and how they achieve those accomplishments, especially when they encounter the same barriers that stymie the progress of many similar schools. In this chapter, we provide a brief overview of what we have learned. Specifically, we depict the elements that make the greatest difference in schools where all student groups excel. As well, we delineate how the elements work together to generate impressive learning results for all student groups. Then, in the following chapters (2 through 7), we will discuss each element in greater detail, describing how leadership teams worked together to develop and position each element within a system that worked to lead all student groups to excel. Finally, in Chapter 8, we will discuss the role district leaders play in supporting the success of school leadership teams.

# The Gears That Drive Success for All Student Groups

In schools that achieve remarkable learning results for all student groups, we find six interlocking elements functioning as gears that drive success for all students. Gears are wheels with teeth. When properly aligned, the teeth of one gear mesh with the teeth of another in a way that transfers energy and facilitates predictable movement. In compound gear systems, multiple gears are attached to the same shaft and rotate smoothly when the gear teeth are carefully aligned. The gears interact to transfer torque and rotational speed and maximize outcomes by efficiently transferring energy. Increased efficiency is especially important when the work to be accomplished is challenging (e.g., pedaling a heavy bicycle uphill or preparing middle school students to succeed in high school mathematics, even when they enter middle school without mastery of whole number operations). In other words, gears can help us work smarter, not just harder. Figure 1.1 portrays six gears found in schools that achieve outstanding learning results for all student groups. The structure of each gear, their alignment, and the way the gears work together to maximize the efficiency of everyone's efforts can propel schools to impressive successes for students who historically have not been served well.

*Figure 1.1* What Drives Change in Schools Where All Student Groups Excel

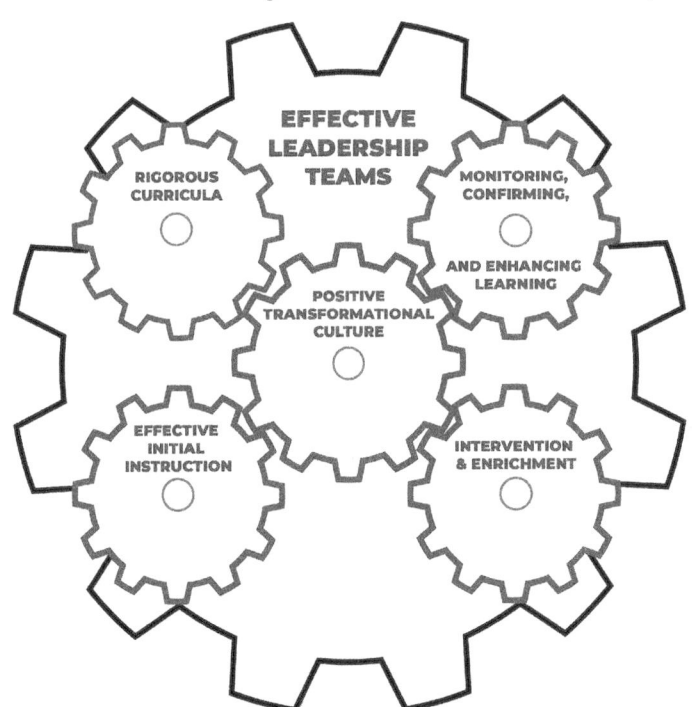

## *Effective Leadership Team*

Figure 1.1 illustrates how an effective leadership team is an input gear. This is the gear to which the input force or torque is applied. It drives the other gears in the train. When leadership teams work effectively, stakeholders (including teachers, support staff, parents, students, and administrators) are much more likely to perceive improvement efforts as coherent, purposeful, and cohesive. For example, when Principal Alonso (see Vignette A) brought teacher teams together to identify the most critical academic standards and determine what students needed to understand to demonstrate deep understanding of those standards, she started to galvanize a shared commitment that drove improvement efforts for over a decade. Similarly, when Principal White (see Vignette B) challenged teacher teams and student teams to identify strategies for changing the school's dismal outcomes on district assessments, they helped establish a unity of purpose that has influenced continuous improvement efforts for years.

The lack of an effective leadership team can hinder the movement of all other gears by slowing, stopping, or reversing progress toward better learning outcomes for all students. When the team leadership gear is moving well, all the other gears are more likely to move more smoothly. When the gear is stuck (i.e., the leadership team is ineffective or non-existent), it is less likely that other gears will move, even when stakeholders exert substantial effort.

In schools that achieve outstanding learning outcomes for all student groups, effective leadership teams accomplish the following important changes:

1) **Stakeholders share the belief that all student groups they serve can and will excel.** School leadership teams are effective when they persistently model their belief in the capacity of all student groups to excel and lead others to express and act upon the same belief (Johnson, Uline, & Munro, 2023, p. 130).

2) **All student groups and all stakeholder groups feel heard and valued.** Effective leadership teams listen to all student groups and all stakeholder groups in ways that inspire trust in the leadership's positive intents (Johnson et al., 2023, p. 151).

3) **Stakeholders believe and value the school's commitment to the success of all student groups.** Effective two-way communication leads all stakeholders to believe school leaders are committed to finding ways to ensure the success of all student groups (Johnson et al., 2023, p. 176).

4) **All personnel understand their roles in moving the six gears that drive success for all students.** School leadership teams are effective when they lead stakeholders to a common, clear understanding about what must happen to ensure the success of all student groups while simultaneously building each individual's sense of responsibility for contributing to those efforts and for supporting their colleagues in pursuing those efforts (Theokas, González, Manriquez, & Johnson, 2019, p. 46).

5) **Stakeholders benefit from powerful systems of support.** School leadership teams are effective when they establish systems of support that lead stakeholders to believe they experience abundant support that empowers them to contribute successfully to efforts for ensuring the success of all student groups (Johnson, Uline, & Perez, 2017, p. 119).

6) **Stakeholders experience collective and individual efficacy.** Effective leadership teams lead school personnel to believe they are part of a team that will make a powerful difference in the lives of students (Johnson et al., 2023, p. 130). The power of the team enhances each individual's feeling of efficacy.

7) **Progress is monitored continuously.** School leadership teams are effective when they continuously monitor the movement of all six gears in ways that maximize the continuous progress of all student groups toward excellent learning outcomes.

Chapter 2 will provide more examples, descriptions, and guides that emphasize **how** you and your colleagues can develop an effective leadership team that facilitates the movement of the other five gears. It is important to note, however, that developing an effective leadership team will not lead to outstanding learning outcomes for all student groups unless the leadership team gear influences movement in the five other gears (positive transformational culture; rigorous curricula; effective initial instruction; monitoring, confirming, and enhancing learning; and intervention and enrichment). These five output gears are depicted in Figure 1.1 as smaller gears in the train; however, they deliver the output torque and speed in ways that maximize the likelihood that the school will generate improved learning outcomes for all student groups. Each is discussed briefly in the following, with greater depth in Chapters 2 through 7.

## *Positive Transformational Culture*

At the center of Figure 1.1, depicting the heart of highly effective schools, is the gear that represents a positive transformational culture. This gear is central to the success of all student groups, but it is particularly central to the success of student groups that historically have been underserved. This gear represents two school-wide accomplishments of leadership teams in America's best schools.

1) **A positive, transformational culture for all student groups.** First, leadership teams developed, nurtured, and sustained a pervasive culture that positively transformed how students perceived the likelihood of their success, in school and in life. Students from all groups achieved at higher levels, in part, because school personnel interacted with them (and led students to interact with each other) in ways that led students to see themselves as respected and respectful citizens of their school and community; thoughtful, engaged scholars who could understand and master challenging academic content; and current and future leaders in their classroom, school, community, and world. Students from all groups felt emotionally and physically safe at school; they believed their presence at school was valued; they believed that adults sought to learn and respond appropriately to their perspectives, insights, and concerns; they believed school personnel took the time to teach them how to succeed socially and academically; and they saw that their efforts to engage in learning activities consistently resulted in greater understanding of important concepts and skills (Johnson, 2019, p. 141). In sum, students who might have previously seen themselves as unsuccessful at school came to see themselves as successful scholars who loved learning.

2) **A positive, transformational culture for all school personnel.** In a parallel manner, leadership teams developed, nurtured, and sustained a positive culture that helped transform how school personnel perceived themselves individually and collectively. School personnel (regardless of title, responsibilities, or years of experience) felt emotionally and

physically safe at school; they believed their presence at school was valued; they believed that school leaders and other colleagues sought to learn and respond appropriately to their perspectives, insights, and concerns; they believed school leaders deliberately structured opportunities to help them succeed professionally; and they saw that their efforts to engage in professional learning activities were consistently rewarded as they achieved greater successes with their students and those successes were acknowledged and celebrated (Johnson et al., 2019, p. 141). Because of a positive, transformational culture, school personnel who might previously have been disengaged or even oppositional began to see themselves as respected, valued, committed, and intelligent educators who could work together in ways that improved the trajectory of students' lives.

When YMLA first opened, Principal White recognized that many of the young men he served had experienced far more academic frustration than academic success. As well, he knew that the academic frustrations had often led to behavioral frustrations that prompted students to conclude they were neither valued nor appreciated at school. Some students might have believed that school was a place where they were being detained until they were old enough to opt out. Some might have believed that adults at school had no sincere interest in helping them succeed. Building a positive transformational culture that led all students to see themselves as capable scholars, thoughtful leaders, and constructive citizens was central to the school's success.

While Principal Alonso sought to elevate rigor and improve instruction at Horace Mann, she realized that those efforts were not likely to be successful without the active involvement of teams of educators. She understood that the school's success depended upon the development of a culture in which a critical mass of educators believed that their insights, perspectives, and experience were valued and respected. She worked to create a culture in which educators felt like they were part of a powerful team that could work together to create outstanding learning outcomes for all students. The efforts to develop a positive transformational culture for school personnel complemented efforts to create a positive transformational culture for all student groups at Horace Mann.

Our observations of America's best schools have led us to conclude that school personnel are not likely to build a culture for their students (especially for their students who have historically been underserved) that is more positive and transformational than the culture leaders build for all school personnel. These two accomplishments are coupled aspects of the same gear, because they stem from the same ethos that respects the capacity of individuals to grow, learn, and improve when they are immersed in a culture that acknowledges and celebrates their capacity to grow, learn, and improve.

In the absence of a positive transformational culture, energy is much less likely to flow sufficiently to cause other gears to turn. School personnel may comply with directives, but they are unlikely to invest the energy necessary to ensure that curricular or instructional initiatives will achieve their potential. Students who have historically felt disengaged will probably continue to sit in classrooms and participate to the extent they feel compelled; however, they are likely to remain disengaged and refrain from investing the effort needed to ensure their success. Chapter 3 will describe in depth the power of a positive transformational culture and explain how leadership teams can unleash such a power to help them improve learning outcomes for all their students.

## *Rigorous Curricula*

Even when the school culture helps all student groups transform their perceptions of themselves as scholars, leaders, and citizens and even when the culture helps school personnel transform their image of themselves as a powerful professional team who can change the trajectory of the lives of all students, outcomes are not likely to improve substantially if classes only rehash lower-level concepts and skills that students learned in prior years. What content must your students master to be convinced they are intelligent scholars who are capable of learning the necessary concepts or skills to achieve their academic, career, and civic goals? In NCUST award-winning schools, leadership teams supported educators in elevating the rigor of what they taught in ways that helped transform how students perceived themselves as scholars. Students from all groups were proud when they saw themselves understanding challenging concepts and skills, and they were eager to learn even more. To set this important gear in motion, educators accomplished three important school-wide shifts:

1) **Agreements about critical concepts/skills to be mastered by all students.** First, educators agreed to ensure their students would master a small set of concepts/skills that students, families, community members, and educators within the school, as well as educators beyond the school, would perceive as academically rigorous and intellectually challenging (Johnson et al., 2017, p. 12). This meant that often teachers did not try to teach students all state standards! Educators who taught the same course or grade level committed to helping students master the concepts/skills that would be most important to their future academic progress in school and the concepts/skills that would be most important to their future progress in life (horizontal alignment).

2) **Commitments to lead all students toward mastering of the critical concepts/skills.** Second, educators agreed to strive to lead all their students to master the rigorous concepts and skills they selected. Often, they did so in a gradual manner, breaking complex concepts and skills into multiple lessons that gave students real opportunities to develop deep understandings. Instead of rushing to "cover" everything, teachers planned lessons to ensure that students developed deep understandings of the most important concepts/skills.

3) **Vertical alignment of critical concepts and skills.** Additionally, educators collaborated vertically across grade levels (in most elementary schools) and across courses (within secondary school departments) to ensure that the concepts and skills selected flowed logically in ways that maximized the likelihood of students' continued success as they moved from one grade to the next or one course to the next (Johnson et al., 2019, pp. 143–144).

Leaders at Horace Mann Elementary recognized that if they continued to act as independent contractors who retreated to their classrooms and addressed the standards they individually wanted to teach, they would not increase the likelihood that all their students would become proficient readers. Similarly, they recognized that there was not enough time in the day nor enough days in the year to teach all literacy and math standards well. Teachers recognized that they needed to agree upon curricula that were both guaranteed (available to all students, regardless of the teacher to whom they were assigned) and viable (sufficiently limited in scope such that all teachers would have a reasonable opportunity to lead all student groups to mastery) (Marzano, 2003).

When the rigorous curricula gear is moving efficiently, school personnel are always thinking strategically about how they will lead all student groups to demonstrate understanding and mastery of rigorous academic standards. Attention to the rigorous curricula gear will transfer purpose and energy to the effective instruction gear; the monitoring, confirming and enhancing learning gear; and the intervention and enrichment gear. Chapter 4 will include more specific examples of how leadership teams can work together to elevate curricular rigor for every student group.

## Effective Initial Instruction

Effective instruction is instruction that results in students mastering the rigorous concepts and skills they need to learn to pursue their academic, civic, and career goals successfully. If instruction does not lead a group of students to master critical, rigorous concepts and skills, instruction for those students is not effective.

In many schools in America, this gear barely moves or moves in only a fraction of classrooms. Many teachers, for many years, have used the same instructional approaches that have not worked well to improve learning results for large percentages of their students. In some schools, leaders blame teachers for the lack of improvement; however, in NCUST award-winning schools, instead of casting blame, leaders examined and then refined the systems or routines that perpetuated ineffective practices or inhibited the implementation of more effective practices. To ensure the school-wide improvement of the initial instruction provided to students, leadership teams worked to accomplish the following important shifts.

1) **Limited focus to a few key instructional practices.** Teams did not seek to change everything about the delivery of instruction. Instead, they selected and limited attention to a few key instructional practices that had a high likelihood of generating improved learning outcomes for their students. Teams emphasized a focus on teaching practices that would either a) lead all students to feel valued and capable; b) strengthen the focus on what students needed to understand/master;

c) promote clarity about lesson intent, design, language, strategic thinking, and assessment; d) check and appropriately respond to student understanding; e) connect learning to the backgrounds, cultures, prior knowledge, and interests of students; f) ensure students developed fluidity with the language associated with the concepts/skills being taught; g) ensure that independent practice was likely to be successful for all students; or h) lead students to love learning (Johnson et al., 2019).

2) **Developed a common understanding of the key practices.** Before racing to implement selected key instructional practices, teams worked to build a shared understanding of the practices, what they looked like when implemented well, how they were different from more common practices, and why they were likely to improve learning results, especially for student groups who historically had not succeeded at their school (Johnson et al., 2019, p. 140).

3) **Celebrated teacher efforts to implement the key practices.** Instead of bashing teachers for failing to utilize the key practices, both teacher leaders and administrative leaders acknowledged and celebrated teacher efforts to implement the key practices and nurtured a school-wide sense of enthusiasm for strengthening implementation (Johnson et al., 2017, pp. 95–98).

4) **Provided teachers abundant support for implementing key practices.** By sustaining attention (for months and often for years) on building a few key instructional practices, leaders helped teachers believe they enjoyed abundant support that would enable them to implement the selected key practices in ways that would result in great learning outcomes for their students (Johnson et al., 2017).

At both YMLA and Horace Mann Elementary, leaders consistently focused on a few key instructional practices over multiple years. The leaders of both schools recognized that improving teachers' initial instructional practices required the development of trust. Teachers had to believe that the instructional practices leaders prioritized were likely to help them improve their students' learning outcomes. Teachers had to believe that leaders were not going to shift instructional priorities with every new fad. Teachers had to see the logical, transparent connection between the concepts and skills their students needed to master, the quality of the initial instruction they provided, and the results their students generated on aligned assessments. The effective initial instruction gear is discussed in greater detail in Chapter 5.

## Monitoring, Confirming, and Enhancing Learning

Often, assessments administered in schools don't mesh explicitly with the specific concepts and skills teachers endeavored to teach their students. Often assessment does not monitor or confirm the extent to which students learned the specific concepts and skills teachers believe they taught. The lack of alignment can cause educational improvement gears to slow or even grind to a halt. How can assessment increase the likelihood that students understand and master rigorous curricula? How can teachers' formal and informal assessments help them enhance the effectiveness of their instruction? How can classroom assessments help all student groups transform how they see themselves as academically talented and capable? In America's best schools, monitoring, confirming, and enhancing learning is an important gear that connects with other gears to generate improved learning outcomes for all student groups.

In NCUST award-winning schools, leadership teams focused on leading their students to master the concepts and skills most important to students' success in school and in life (the rigorous curricula gear). As well, leadership teams supported their colleagues in providing effective initial instruction designed to ensure their students were likely to acquire deep understandings of the critical concepts and skills (the effective initial instruction gear). These important efforts would have been incomplete if there were not efforts to monitor, confirm, and enhance learning. As leadership teams endeavored to transform how students perceived their capacity to learn and achieve, they supported teachers in designing formal and informal strategies that gave students unambiguous feedback about the rigorous concepts they had mastered and what they were yet to master. Similarly, as leadership teams worked to transform how educators perceived their ability to teach the various groups of students they served, strategies were designed to provide educators concrete evidence that they could teach and their students could learn rigorous academic concepts and skills.

In many American schools, there is a glut of assessment; however, there might not be any assessment that is aligned in a way that helps teachers know what students understood and what students didn't understand about the specific concept or skill they tried to teach. There might not be any assessment that tells teachers, "As of Friday, 16 of your students demonstrated they understood these three concepts well. The 16 students could explain the concepts and describe how they interrelated; while your other 14 students could not explain at least one of the three concepts."

Monitoring, confirming, and enhancing learning is rare in most schools. Teachers know they must administer assessments. They know results will be shared with them at some point; however, they often don't know why specific assessment items were chosen, how the items relate to the concepts they were asked to teach, or how to use the results to best enhance learning for students who did not demonstrate understanding. Further, they don't know how to use the assessment results to continue building the knowledge and skills of students who successfully demonstrated mastery. To move the monitoring, confirming, and enhancing learning gear effectively, leadership teams worked to ensure they accomplished the following:

1) **Assessments communicated to students and parents how mastery of specific concepts/skills would be assessed.** Assessments were aligned well enough to communicate clearly (to teachers, students, administrators, and parents) how students would be expected to demonstrate their understanding and mastery of the specific challenging academic standards that were the focus of instruction (Johnson et al., 2019, p. 144).

2) **Teachers who taught the same content used the same assessments.** To ensure all students (school-wide) advanced toward mastery of specific agreed-upon concepts and skills, assessments were common to all classrooms at the same grade or all classrooms that taught the same course (Johnson et al., 2019, p. 144).

3) **Teachers used assessment results to share how well students mastered specific concepts/skills.** Assessment results were communicated transparently (to teachers, students, administrators, and parents), highlighting what students understood and what students had not yet mastered related to the specific agreed-upon concepts and skills (DuFour & Marzano, 2011, pp. 121–122).

4) **Teachers used assessment results to respond strategically to students' learning needs.** Assessment results were used by teaching teams to respond to students' specific needs, build upon students' strengths, and improve subsequent initial instruction (DuFour & Marzano, 2011, pp. 132–133).

When teachers committed to teach all their students the same critical concepts and skills and then gauged students' understanding and mastery using common, aligned assessments, they challenged themselves to improve the quality of instruction they provided their students. At Horace Mann Elementary, teachers worked together to create common formative assessments to determine how well students throughout the grade level were progressing toward mastery of the academic concepts and skills they had prioritized. Similarly, at YMLA, Principal White explained that educators at the school were able to achieve greater "transparency" when assessments aligned clearly and consistently with the concepts they wanted their students to learn. He shared, "The tie between the classroom learning objective, the activities of the lesson, and the assessment provided was clear to everyone. Teachers were more likely to accept responsibility for learning results when there was a clear, transparent connection between learning expectations, lesson activities, and assessment."

The monitoring, confirming, and enhancing learning gear added coherence to improvement efforts by ensuring school-wide alignment between rigorous curricular concepts and skills, the assessments used to measure mastery of those concepts and skills, and the instructional approaches used to ensure that all students were able to demonstrate mastery. Chapter 6 will explore specific strategies schools used to maximize the impact of monitoring, confirming, and enhancing learning.

## Effective Intervention and Enrichment

In America's best schools, effective initial instruction was a powerful tool for generating better learning results; however, even with outstanding initial instruction, educators recognized that some students needed more support. As a result, leadership teams worked diligently to establish the sixth gear, effective intervention and enrichment.

In many typical American schools, teachers introduce a concept or skill, provide some initial instruction, conduct an assessment, and enter a grade into a gradebook. Often, teachers don't feel they have time for intervention or enrichment. Conversely, in some schools, students are assigned "intervention" for an entire semester or year. In contrast, in America's best schools, intervention and enrichment complement the other five gears in a way that makes student understanding and mastery a logical consequence of everyone's efforts. Specifically, teams have worked to accomplish the following:

1) **Intervention and enrichment are laser-focused on specific concepts and skills.** Sessions are tailored to build upon what students have demonstrated they know, correct students' specific misconceptions, and build the thinking processes that will serve students well as they approach similar problems throughout their lives (Theokas et al., 2019, p. 141).

2) **Intervention and enrichment are timely.** To ensure responsivity to what students are thinking about the concept/skill being taught, intervention and enrichment occur almost immediately after formal or informal assessment (Theokas et al., 2019, p. 142).

3) **Intervention and enrichment are provided by trained personnel.** Educators need to be able to assess student thinking, identify both thinking strengths and misconceptions, and model excellent teaching practices. To date, we have not observed any software or hardware with greater capacity to understand how a student is thinking than a committed teacher.

4) **Intervention and enrichment are often collaboratively designed.** Teacher teams develop lessons that are likely to build upon the most effective strategies for teaching key concepts and skills (Johnson et al., 2023, pp. 136–137).

5) **Intervention and enrichment lead students to love learning.** Educators provide opportunities for real-world application of concepts/skills in ways that maximize relevance (Johnson et al., 2023, pp. 184–186).

At YMLA, Principal White emphasized that moving students forward when they had not developed understanding of key concepts and skills served neither the student nor the school. He explained:

I tell teachers we are not moving on until we have mastered the content. Learning is built upon foundations. If you move on without establishing a strong foundation, you can't expect success down the road. I know the district has a scope and sequence chart, and I know they tell us to stick to it, but if the young men aren't learning, we don't stick to it. Our teachers know they're not going to feel the heat from me. But when students have mastered it, then it's time to move on. Or if kids already know the content, don't spend too much time on it. Let's move on and teach them things they don't know.

(Johnson et al., 2023, pp. 118–119)

At Horace Mann Elementary, in grade-level collaboration meetings, teachers discussed student assessment results and decided next steps to ensure that students mastered the concepts they worked diligently to teach. Often, they organized follow-up lessons to include small-group sessions during which they helped students deconstruct their misconceptions and build deeper, more accurate understandings. They organized meaningful activities that provided students relevant opportunities to apply the concepts they were learning to real-life situations.

In America's best schools, intervention is not a separate track that reduces the likelihood that some students access challenging academic concepts and skills (Oakes, 2005). In schools where students are scheduled into "intervention" as a course or daily routine, often the intervention gear works in opposition to the rigorous curricula gear. As students spend more time in intervention, they are less likely to access the challenging concepts they need to learn to succeed in the next grade or the next course. In NCUST award-winning schools, the intervention and enrichment gear works continuously to maximize the likelihood that all students will continue to master rigorous criteria. Chapter 7 will provide more examples of how leadership teams developed effective intervention and enrichment.

In sum, the effective leadership team serves as the input gear (teeth) and ensures that all other gears – positive transformational culture; rigorous curricula; effective initial instruction; monitoring, confirming, and enhancing learning; and intervention and enrichment – work in harmony to transmit motion and power, in ways that promote the success of all students. Without an effective leadership team, it is difficult to coordinate and sustain the elements.

# What It Is and What It Isn't: The Gears That Drive Success for All Students

**(X) What It Isn't: Claiming to Have Established an Outstanding School While Ignoring the Lack of Success of Some Groups of Students (Even Small Groups of Students)**

> Some leaders point to overall student data as evidence of success and ignore evidence suggesting some student groups achieve far less social or academic success. When evidence of a lack of success emerges for some students, leaders downplay (or fail to refute others who downplay) the evidence by blaming characteristics of the students or their families, small numbers of students in the group, issues with prior schools, or other external factors. They fail to challenge themselves to build upon their successes in ways that will ensure the success of all the students they have the privilege to serve.

**(✓) What It Is: Focusing Upon Ensuring the Success of All Student Groups**

> Leaders in America's best schools embrace the goal of ensuring the social and academic success of all students (regardless of how students are labeled, categorized, or grouped). If the school generates less evidence of success for one student group, leaders act with a moral imperative. They recognize and articulate the need to improve systems in ways that will lead every group of students to success. Leaders acknowledge and celebrate the progress of each student group in ways that inspire hope and a sense of efficacy.

**(X) What It Isn't: Assuming That Addressing One or Two Gears Will Be Sufficient**

> Some leaders invest all their energy into improving one or two gears and act as if the other gears are not necessary. For example, some leaders will focus exclusively on building a powerful, positive transformational culture but not pay attention to the need to elevate curricular rigor or the need to improve the

effectiveness of initial instruction. Attention to one gear may generate important gains; however, the gains might not be sustained, or might be sustained for only certain student groups, if there isn't deliberate effort to ensure that the energy from one gear's movement is transferred to other important gears.

## ✓ What It Is: Persisting in Building Coherent Systems Where All System Elements Work Together to Maximize the Success of All Student Groups

Leaders recognize that ensuring the success of all student groups requires multi-pronged, coordinated, and coherent strategies. They understand that, ultimately, all six gears must work in tandem in ways that maximize the likelihood that every student group will succeed. As well, they recognize that the gears cannot be perfected overnight. Leaders help all stakeholders understand the need for persisting to establish a coherent system where all the gears work smoothly to advance the success of all student groups.

## ✗ What It Isn't: Assuming that Stakeholders Will Need to Be Forced, Manipulated, or Sidestepped in Order to Change Systems in Ways That Will Ensure the Success of All Student Groups

Many leaders passionately aspire to make a positive difference for all the students they serve. Some leaders act as if the best way to achieve the changes they want is to insist upon compliance with their vision. They assume they know how to best move all the gears that influence success for all student groups, and they assume other opinions are grounded in either a disbelief that success is possible or a commitment to sustaining the status quo. Even when those assumptions are correct, leaders rarely succeed by ordering compliance or ignoring different points of view. The most successful leaders clearly and persistently share their beliefs; however, they simultaneously create an environment where others know that their perspectives are heard, considered, and valued; their best ideas are integrated in ways that refine approaches, and their ideas that do not advance the success of all students are respectfully yet clearly rejected.

## ✓ What It Is: Engaging Stakeholders in Building and Moving All the Gears That Drive Student Success

Great leadership teams know their success relies upon their ability to engage the stakeholders upon whom success depends. Continuously, leadership teams help all stakeholders understand that success for all students depends on the school's collective capacity to move all six gears. As well, leadership teams persistently reach out to teachers and support personnel, as well as to students and parents (from all demographic groups) to acquire their perspectives about what is needed, what is working, and how the school might improve. Continuously, leadership teams engage stakeholders in looking at data, identifying challenges, and considering possible solutions. Success is much more likely when everyone has constructed the route to success.

# Tips for Leadership Teams

- Leadership teams should arrange opportunities to help various stakeholder groups understand each of the gears that drive the success of all student groups. Some groups need deeper levels of understanding of the gears than others; however, all stakeholders should understand how the academic and social success of all students can be enhanced through comprehensive efforts to advance all six gears.

- Engage stakeholders in looking at the school's data and noting evidence of successes. Encourage the examination of both summative data (e.g., year-end data) and formative data to identify opportunities to improve the likelihood that every student who enrolls will learn and grow in ways that improve their success in school and their success in life. Generate enthusiasm among all stakeholder groups for building upon the school's strengths by elevating outcomes for student groups that have been less likely to experience school success. Engage stakeholders in exploring how each of the six gears might be strengthened and advanced in ways that will help ensure all student groups at your school are likely to excel.

- As a leadership team, look for ways in which the six gears seemed to be disconnected. In particular, explore possible disconnections for various groups of students. For example, do students with disabilities at your school experience initial instruction that isn't designed to lead them to learn the rigorous curricula that you believe all students need to master? Do students experiencing behavioral issues have a lower likelihood of experiencing effective initial instruction because they are frequently removed from class because of their misbehavior? Determine the reasons for the disconnections and define systems that could help ensure new, powerful, and consistent connections that make the most of everyone's efforts.

- Look for best practices in the school related to the six gears and consider what systems could help make those practices prevalent throughout the school. What training, support, and reinforcement could help islands of excellence become school-wide strengths?

## References

DuFour, R., & Marzano, R. J. (2011). *Leaders of learning: How district, school, and classroom leaders improve student achievement*. Bloomington, IN: Solution Tree.

Johnson, J. F., Uline, C. L., & Munro, S. J. (2023). *When Black students excel: How schools can engage and empower Black students*. New York: Routledge and Taylor & Francis Group.

Johnson, J. F., Uline, C. L., & Perez, L. (2017). *Leadership in America's best urban schools*. New York: Routledge and Taylor & Francis Group.

Johnson, J. F., Uline, C. L., & Perez, L. (2019). *Teaching practices from America's best urban schools: A guide for school and classroom leaders*. New York: Routledge and Taylor & Francis Group.

Marzano, R. J. (2003). *What works in schools: Translating research into action*. Alexandria, VA: ASCD.

Oakes, J. (2005). *Keeping track: How schools structure inequality.* New Haven, CT: Yale University Press.

Theokas, C., González, M. L., Manriquez, C., & Johnson, J. F. (2019). *Five practices for improving the success of Latino students: A guide for secondary school leaders.* New York: Routledge and Taylor & Francis Group.

# 2 Effective Leadership Teams

> **Voices of Students and Parents From America's Best Schools**
>
> "It's the support system they have here. The teachers, the administration, the counselors, everybody who works here. I've never seen anybody who works here who hasn't been a support for a student."
> – Parent of a student at Veterans Memorial Early College High School, Brownsville, TX
>
> "All the adults here work like they're part of the same team. They try to get all of us kids to succeed in achieving whatever we want to achieve in life. The staff works together to get all of us across the goal line."
> – Gabriela, student at Veterans Memorial Early College High School, Brownsville, TX
>
> "I attended P.S. 249 from Pre-K to 5th grade. I struggled with socializing, speaking up, talking to peers, making friends, and talking about, honestly, anything. I have overcome these challenges with the help of teachers, peers, and administrators at P.S. 249. My teachers helped me by creating a warm learning environment, placing me in small groups, and talking to me during SEL [social emotional learning]. I no longer struggle with socializing or sharing my voice. My peers at P.S. 249 helped me by talking to me and accepting me as a friend. The staff at the Caton School are so caring, welcoming, and inviting. I worked closely with Principal Brown, the assistant principals, and my guidance counselor on important issues and projects. I gave speeches during assemblies, made the afternoon announcements, created flyers, prepared for school events,

and met with my amazing and very kind principal who recently completed her doctoral defense and is officially recognized as Dr. Brown. I was promoted in spring 2023 and I now attend J.H.S 259, William McKinley Middle School. I am proud to say that I am in all honors classes. I am a confident leader who will continue to speak up for myself and others."

— Anisah, former student at P.S. 249, the Caton School

## VIGNETTE C: Veterans Memorial Early College High School, Brownsville Independent School District, Brownsville, Texas

**WON NCUST'S AMERICA'S BEST SCHOOL AWARD IN 2016, 2017, AND 2024**

*When describing their school, several teachers at Veterans Memorial Early College High School emphasized "teamwork." Teachers explained that they worked together to make sure that all students had opportunities to experience success in athletics, the arts, rigorous career and technology education programs, and challenging academic programs, including a vast array of advanced placement courses and courses that offer dual enrollment credit with local post-secondary institutions. Teachers explained that, as a team, they tried to ensure that every student experienced success, including students with disabilities, students who are newcomers from Mexico or other countries, students who struggled in middle school, and students who aspire to attend some of the nation's most prestigious colleges and universities.*

*Teachers expressed excitement about being part of a team that was willing to do more to help students experience success. Teachers talked about how they worked collaboratively with special education specialists and bilingual education specialists to help ensure all students experienced success in their rigorous courses. Teachers expressed pride in their efforts to provide Saturday academies and afterschool tutorials to help ensure students succeeded in mastering challenging academic concepts. As well, teachers talked about how they enjoyed posting problems and exemplary student work outside their classrooms. They* enjoyed taking students on "gallery walks" to showcase the hard work and brilliance of Veterans' students.

An important aspect of the teamwork at Veterans was the commitment to ensuring every student was on the road to success. Teachers made sure students who missed classes because of extra-curricular competitions had opportunities to access information from important lessons. Some teams of teachers met five days a week to plan lessons and track how well students were demonstrating mastery of important concepts. Teachers tracked the progress of students to make sure they were mastering the concepts and skills needed to pass the state's assessment that allowed them to begin earning post-secondary course credit. Team members invested time and energy in ways that led to more student successes. Ultimately, more student successes led more team members to invest even more time and energy in ways that led even more students to succeed.

---

## VIGNETTE D: P.S. 249, The Caton School, New York City Department of Education, Brooklyn, New York

**WON NCUST'S AMERICA'S BEST SCHOOL AWARD IN 2023**

*When Elise Brown was appointed as the third principal in three years to lead Brooklyn's P.S. 249 (the Caton School), the school was grappling with low test scores and a demoralized staff. Eighty-five percent of third graders were performing at the lowest level on New York City's reading and math exams. Dr. Brown knew she needed the support of a great team of teachers to generate substantial improvements in teaching and learning. She believed she needed to find ways to empower teachers so they might work together to help all students learn important academic concepts and skills.*

Principal Brown identified a group of experienced teachers and coached them to lead their colleagues in weekly professional learning communities (PLCs). First, the group of experienced teacher leaders worked with their peers to identify the most essential learning standards and create pre-assessment items that were directly aligned to specific concepts and skills associated with those standards. After administering the pre-assessment to students, teachers reconvened to analyze student work and take note of the concepts students had already learned, as well as the concepts students needed to learn. Then, the teachers worked together to select *instructional strategies that had a high likelihood of helping their students develop clear understandings of the concepts they needed to learn. Often, the more experienced teachers modeled the selected strategies for the rest of their team. In a supportive, collaborative environment, newer teachers had opportunities to practice the strategies and receive useful feedback. The support helped teachers improve the quality and effectiveness of their initial instruction and helped reduce disparities in student performance, regardless of teacher experience levels.*

*Despite their hard work, test scores initially dropped, leaving many educators disheartened. Principal Brown, however, persisted. She knew she was building collective efficacy among the team. Teachers were growing confident in their ability to apply pre- and post-assessment cycles and adjust their instructional strategies accordingly. They also became more open to modeling these strategies for one another. As they regularly observed their peers, high-quality initial instructional practices spread throughout the school. Teachers were collaborating frequently and learning from each other. Over time, teachers at P.S. 249 came to believe in their collective ability to educate their students. Dr. Brown and her team of administrators and teacher leaders transformed the way teachers perceived their ability to help students from all demographic groups master challenging academic standards. They transformed the way parents perceived their children's future and the way students perceived themselves as scholars and citizens.*

---

Many researchers have noted that outstanding schools have outstanding principals (Edmonds, 1979; Hattie, 2023; Leithwood, Louis, Anderson, & Wahlstrom, 2004; Lezotte & Snyder, 2011; Marzano, Waters, & McNulty, 2005). What may be less obvious in the research literature, yet abundantly obvious in the schools that have earned NCUST's America's Best Schools Award, is that outstanding principals do not lead single-handedly. Both Veterans Memorial Early College High School in Brownsville, Texas (as described in Vignette C), and the Caton School in Brooklyn, New York (as described in Vignette D), benefitted from outstanding principals who were wise enough to recognize their chances of achieving success for all student groups would be greatly enhanced through the development of effective leadership teams.

Effective leadership is more than the management of student behavior, facilities, and finances; more than the management of relationships among adults; and more than the pursuit of innovative ideas (Robinson, 2011). Instead, "the ruler for judging the effectiveness of educational leadership is its impact on the learning and achievement of students for whom the leader is responsible" (Robinson, 2011, p. 4). We argue similarly that effective leadership teams are those that improve the learning and achievement of students, especially those groups of students who historically have not been served well.

Outstanding principals build, inspire, and empower leadership teams to formulate, align, and refine the gears that drive success for all students. Leadership teams may differ in their size and composition. The frequency with which they meet and collaborate may also vary. The leadership teams who serve NCUST's award-winning schools, however, are alike in what they seek to accomplish. At these schools, leadership teams remain laser focused on ensuring the success of all student groups. This chapter explores this primary concern and provides suggestions for optimizing the effectiveness of leadership teams.

## What Effective Leadership Teams Seek to Accomplish

Many schools have an entity they call their "leadership team." Unfortunately, in too many schools, the leadership team does not play a pivotal role in improving the success of all student groups. In this section, we describe what leadership teams in NCUST's award-winning schools seek to accomplish that sets them apart from more typical school leadership teams. By considering what effective leadership teams seek to accomplish, you can determine whom to engage on your school's leadership team, how to structure the leadership team's work, and how to build the capacity of the leadership team members so they are likely to maximize the success of all student groups at your school.

### Effective Leadership Teams Build a School-Wide Shared Belief in the Capacity of All Student Groups to Excel

Through their own professional learning experiences (e.g., reading about high-performing schools, visiting the classrooms of teachers who generate excellent learning outcomes for historically underserved students, analyzing teaching practices that helped students produce outstanding work), effective leadership teams continuously strengthen a shared belief in their capacity to help all student groups excel (Johnson, Uline, & Perez, 2017). Additionally, their decisions and actions affirm this shared belief in ways that generate a positive sense of possibility among parents and a sense of efficacy among students who might have rarely felt efficacious about academics. In all leadership team decisions and actions, school personnel see and hear an unwavering belief in the capacity of all student groups to excel. This enthusiasm often leads personnel to redouble individual and collective efforts in improving learning outcomes. On the other hand, the enthusiasm leads some disbelievers to look for other places to work.

## Effective Leadership Teams Multiply the Likelihood That All Student Groups and All Stakeholder Groups Will Feel Heard and Valued

In outstanding schools, leadership teams were often deployed to spend time listening to individuals and groups of students, parents, school staff members, and community members. Whether through empathy interviews, surveys, focus groups, Zoom meetings (or similar technology), visits to community events, home visits, or other strategies, leadership teams helped people believe their ideas were important and their perspectives were valued.

According to Aronson (2008), when educators simply ask students about their opinions and feelings, they open opportunities to dismantle stereotypes and increase the likelihood that all students feel valued at school. He explained:

> The everyday antiracist "move" I rely upon is to cultivate a mindset of insatiable curiosity about my students as individuals: who they are, the experiences they have had, what they think about things, and how they think. Curiosity is the diametrical opposite of stereotyping and prejudice, the assumption that you know who a person is, what they think, or how they will act simply because you know what category they belong to.
> 
> (Aronson, 2008, pp. 67–68)

Often, when we interviewed students at NCUST award-winning schools, students described how teachers and administrators frequently asked them questions such as, "What do you think about this program? How did this strategy work for you? Could you relate to the characters in that novel? What could we do to make this schedule work better for you?" Similarly, parents would tell us how teachers and administrators regularly reached out to them and asked, "What are we doing that is working for your child? What could we do better? How can we help improve your child's chances for success?" When we interviewed school personnel, we often heard teachers, paraprofessionals, counselors and other personnel explain how school leaders asked them, "What do you think about this schedule, this product, this approach, or this idea? What could we do to help you succeed with your students?" Often, leaders sought answers to these questions by reaching out in a sincere way to gather input directly from the individuals or groups who could best provide the perspective needed. In particular, we noted leadership teams reaching out to learn from and about students who struggled in classes, who sometimes experienced behavioral challenges, who did not speak English at home, who were deemed "chronically absent," or who were not likely to graduate on time. As a result of these efforts, students who might have otherwise felt ignored, or even unwanted, came to believe that their teachers and administrators cared about them and wanted them to succeed. These students (and their parents) were much more likely to invest effort, time, and energy, because they believed their school leaders cared.

## *Effective Leadership Teams Communicate the Reasons for Decisions in Ways That Lead Stakeholders to Believe and Value the School's Commitment to the Success of All Student Groups*

Listening to others is essential but often not sufficient. Often stakeholders need a reason to believe that what they shared was heard and actually influenced a decision. Leadership team members at NCUST award-winning schools reached agreement about how decisions would be communicated. Team members assumed responsibility for helping the groups they represented understand how decisions were responsive to the input provided, how decisions would be implemented to maximize the likelihood of better outcomes for all student groups, and how decisions would be revisited after a reasonable time period to consider possible refinements. In less effective schools, stakeholders might hear, "The principal is making us do it this way," as the only rationale for decisions. In effective schools, leadership teams shared responsibility for communicating the rationale for decisions in ways that helped stakeholders know their concerns were heard and appreciated. Over time, stakeholders came to trust that the continued improvement of learning outcomes for all student groups remained a critical consideration in all decisions.

When leadership teams effectively communicate the reasoning behind decisions, as they relate to the success of all student groups, stakeholders are likely to believe in the importance of the goals they are working to achieve. If stakeholders perceive they are being asked to pursue a goal that is trivial, bureaucratic, or not in the best interest of students, stakeholders will be less likely to commit the effort required to ensure the desired outcomes are achieved (Johnson et al., 2017). If stakeholders believe leaders are asking them to do something that is not likely to advance the success of certain student groups, stakeholders concerned about those student groups are not likely to commit their effort wholeheartedly. Stakeholders are more likely to invest the time and energy necessary to change their practices when they perceive the goal is worthwhile because its fulfillment will positively influence students' lives.

## *Effective Leadership Teams Lead All Personnel to Understand Their Roles in Moving the Six Gears That Drive Success for All Students*

In NCUST award-winning schools, school personnel see clearly what they need to do to improve learning outcomes for their students. They don't wait, hoping for "better" students to appear in their classrooms. Neither do they methodically continue to implement unsuccessful practices, hoping for miraculously different results. In contrast, effective leadership teams lead school personnel to understand clearly and logically what they must do (individually and collectively) to drive success for all students.

As emphasized in Vignette D, Principal Brown and her team of experienced teachers led Caton School educators to develop clear, common understandings of the critical concepts and skills their students needed to master in order to maximize their choices as they advanced through school and life (rigorous curricula). As well, they helped ensure that Caton School teachers had common ways of determining the extent to which students had learned the critical concepts and skills (monitoring, confirming, and enhancing learning).

As described in Vignette C, Veterans Memorial teachers met often (sometimes every day) to plan and implement excellent, engaging lessons that maximized the likelihood that all students would achieve mastery of challenging academic concepts (effective initial instruction). Additionally, based on the assumption that some students might need more support, teacher leaders at Veterans worked with the school's administrators to plan and implement effective Saturday academies and afterschool tutorials (effective intervention and enrichment).

Effective leadership teams build clarity among stakeholders regarding what critical efforts must improve (which gears must move, in which direction, toward what end) to ensure excellent learning outcomes for all student groups. Stakeholders must understand how these critical tasks are best implemented. In the absence of such clarity, stakeholders are likely to continue doing the same things they did previously.

In some schools, leaders focus on helping school personnel understand what they should help their students learn (i.e., rigorous curricula). In some schools, leaders focus on helping school personnel understand how to provide lessons that will lead all students to master rigorous curricula (i.e., effective initial instruction, intervention, and enrichment) or how school personnel will know if their students developed mastery of the concepts and skills taught (i.e., monitoring, confirming, and enhancing learning). Rarely, however, do school leadership teams help school personnel understand all these roles in a logical, connected manner. And it is especially rare for leadership teams to help school personnel understand how to pursue all these efforts (rigorous curricula; effective instruction; monitoring, confirming, and enhancing learning; and intervention and enrichment) in a manner that leads all students to perceive themselves as valued, respected, and capable of achieving outstanding academic successes (a positive transformational culture for all student groups). Simultaneously, leadership team efforts should lead all school personnel to understand that part of their role is to support their colleagues in perceiving themselves as valued, respected, and capable members of a powerful professional team that is changing the trajectory of students' lives (a positive transformational culture for all school personnel).

## *Effective Leadership Teams Ensure All Stakeholders, Throughout the School, Perceive That They Benefit From Powerful Systems of Support*

Effective leadership teams ensure that all school personnel believe they have abundant, high-quality support that will lead them to be successful contributors to a professional team that is improving students' lives. Effective leadership teams create systems of support that make all school personnel feel they have a high likelihood of helping their students achieve remarkable academic successes.

At many schools that serve large percentages of students of color, students who meet low-income criteria, or students who speak languages other than English at home, educators feel an urgency to improve learning outcomes for students who historically have not been served well. Teachers at the Caton School and at Veterans Memorial felt a similar urgency; however, they also benefitted from systems of support designed to help them successfully lift their students to new academic heights. Effective leadership teams build a culture in which individuals and groups are likely to accept responsibility for accomplishing their roles in ensuring excellent learning outcomes for all student groups. If stakeholders fear being blamed or embarrassed about their difficulties fulfilling their roles, they are more likely to resist accepting responsibility and are more likely to blame others. In contrast, effective leadership teams insist upon examining disappointments and setbacks through a systemic lens (Johnson et al., 2017). The focus becomes, "How can we improve our systems so that everyone is more likely to accomplish what we want them to accomplish?" For example, when achievement results at the Caton School initially went down after strong efforts by many teachers, Principal Brown and her team of teacher leaders did not look to cast blame. Instead, they looked for opportunities to strengthen their support so that all teachers were more likely to succeed.

Effective leadership teams create a culture that does not expect perfection from anyone. Instead, they create a culture that expects and supports continuous growth and improvement. Effective leadership teams find ways of promoting, identifying, and celebrating growth as school personnel work to improve their practices and move each of the other five gears that drive success for all student groups.

## *Effective Leadership Teams Create the Conditions Within Which Stakeholders Develop a Sense of Individual and Collective Efficacy*

In struggling schools, often school personnel don't believe they have much chance of improving the trajectory of their students' lives. Sometimes, educators believe the best they can do is "manage" until retirement, until the end of the school year, or until Friday. In some schools, educators believe they can reasonably be expected to lead some students to high levels of academic success; however, they honestly don't know how they can be expected to help other students succeed (especially students who historically have not been successful). In contrast, in NCUST award-winning schools, school personnel speak and act with confidence that, together, they have outstanding opportunities to make profound differences in the lives of most (if not all) of their students. Researchers have referred to this phenomenon as collective teacher efficacy.

Collective teacher efficacy is more powerful than socio-economic factors in predicting student achievement in reading and mathematics (Goddard, Hoy, & Hoy, 2000). In fact, a meta-analysis of 85 studies revealed that collective teacher efficacy had a larger effect size on student achievement than almost any other variable (Hattie, 2023). It is not surprising that school leadership teams are most effective when they build a sense of collective efficacy among school personnel (Johnson, Uline, & Munro, 2023).

Building collective efficacy, among teachers and the personnel who support teachers, drives the improvement of learning outcomes for all student groups served, because it influences how personnel perceive their individual and collective mission, that is, the difference they expect to make in the lives of the students they serve. In his examination of the effects of collective efficacy across several social systems that included education, Bandura (2000) found that, "the higher the perceived collective efficacy, the higher the group's motivational investment in their undertakings, the stronger their staying power in the face of impediments and setbacks, and the greater their performance accomplishments" (p. 78).

It is important to note that educators may feel successful and efficacious in one school and feel inconsequential and incapable of ensuring student success in another. For example, in one school, educators may feel efficacious because almost all their students begin the school year at or above grade level, speak English fluently at home, and have parents who can help them understand challenging assignments. In contrast, the same team of educators may doubt their ability to lead their students to excel academically if almost all of the students start the school year below grade level, few have access to additional educational support at home, and many have challenges that teachers are not accustomed to addressing successfully. In many schools, the development of collective efficacy requires sustained time and effort.

At Horace Mann Elementary (Vignette A), leaders realized that teachers needed the opportunity to work in teams to plan new, effective lessons that were likely to help students master very challenging academic standards. At YMLA (Vignette B), teachers needed regular, supportive feedback that helped them logically connect the objectives their students needed to learn, the lesson activities they utilized, and the assessments they designed. As well, teachers needed support in redesigning instruction in ways that were more likely to engage students actively. At the Caton School (Vignette D), leaders realized that teachers needed the support of experienced teachers who could model the practices they were being asked to adopt in their classrooms. At Veterans Memorial (Vignette C), the leadership team knew they needed to find ways beyond the regular school day to meet the needs of students they wanted to succeed in rigorous academic courses, including dual-credit and advanced placement classes.

Leaders build a sense of collective efficacy among teachers to the degree they identify and eliminate the barriers that inhibit efficacy. Effective leadership teams acknowledge that longstanding policies, programs, practices, and routines may interfere with the movement of some or all of the gears that drive student success. Therefore, effective leadership teams assume responsibility for closely examining practices that are rarely questioned at more traditional schools. For example, the leadership team at Veterans Memorial acknowledged that the traditional workday and school week did not provide sufficient time to generate the levels of success they believed their students were capable of achieving. Consequently, they found ways to establish powerful afterschool and Saturday programs. Leadership teams at NCUST award-winning schools constantly challenged themselves to identify and dismantle dysfunctional practices and routines that kept teachers and students from feeling efficacious. As well, they often piloted, monitored, and refined more effective practices that facilitated the efficient movement of all six gears in ways that helped everyone feel a greater sense of efficacy.

## *Effective Leadership Teams Continuously Monitor Implementation in Ways That Improve Both Efforts and Outcomes*

Chenoweth (2009) reported that, in schools where unexpectedly positive learning results were achieved, school personnel continuously monitored their progress. Monitoring was not intended to reprimand, discipline, punish, or negate anyone or anyone's efforts. Instead, the intent was to look for opportunities to grow, improve, refine, build upon, and support everyone and everyone's efforts.

The "gallery walks" at Veteran's Memorial Early College High School were a form of monitoring not designed to find fault but to inspire growth. When the Caton School teachers reconvened after administering common formative assessments, they did so with the primary intent of learning about the teaching practices that helped their colleagues lead students to master challenging concepts and skills. They sought to learn and build upon one another's successes. Effective leadership teams developed a variety of strategies that helped school personnel positively and constructively examine practices, procedures, and routines. They promoted monitoring in ways that did not shame or blame anyone. They created environments that led everyone to feel safe about sharing student work and learning outcomes. They developed an ever-growing sense of collective teacher efficacy by demonstrating how personnel could learn from each other without judging each other, how they could support each other without belittling each other, and how they could offer each other their very best practices and ideas in ways that enriched the entire school.

## Why Establishing Effective Leadership Teams Is Challenging Yet Rewarding

Establishing an effective leadership team that continuously pursues the accomplishments described in this chapter requires considerable time, energy, and focus. The challenges are substantial; however, the rewards are even more substantial. Table 2.1 describes the challenges schools might expect to face, as well as the rewards schools might expect to accrue if they persist in building effective leadership teams.

Table 2.1 Challenges and Rewards of Establishing Effective Leadership Teams

| Issue | The Challenges | The Rewards |
|---|---|---|
| **Leading everyone to feel heard and valued** | Most schools don't have routines that establish time for listening to students or personnel. Sometimes it may seem difficult to make time for acquiring input from stakeholders. | The time expended will yield important information that can improve school processes. Also, the time expended will help convince stakeholders that they are valued. |
| **Leading everyone to feel heard and valued** | Some administrators fear that empowering a leadership team could result in them losing "control." In outstanding schools, administrators find that they are more likely to generate excellent effort and outstanding outcomes when they empower a leadership team that makes everyone feel heard and valued. | Over time, effective teams assume a sense of responsibility for accomplishing necessary changes. Administrators both retain and share responsibility with team members who develop a sense of ownership. |
| **Communicate so that everyone sees how decisions connect with commitments** | Even when leadership teams work together to make decisions, team members often don't assume responsibility for helping their constituents see the rationale behind decisions. All team members must assume responsibility for helping constituents understand how decisions are intended to serve students well. | When all leadership team members assume responsibility for helping constituents understand why and how school-wide decisions were made, stakeholders are more likely to respect and value school-wide decisions. |
| **Building a shared belief in the capacity of all students to excel** | Leadership team members may need support in developing the belief that all students can excel. They may need regular ongoing support if they are to help their colleagues believe that all students can excel. | Efforts to build the capacity of leadership team members can accelerate the progress of an entire school by building a sense of collective efficacy. |

(Continued)

Table 2.1 (Continued)

| Issue | The Challenges | The Rewards |
|---|---|---|
| Leading all personnel to understand their roles in moving the six gears | Often, school personnel feel overwhelmed by the number of important concerns that need their attention. Personnel may want to believe that all students can excel, but they don't know clearly what they need to do to ensure their students succeed. | Effective leadership teams help everyone see a clear, logical path for improving learning outcomes for all groups of students. What felt improbable will feel possible when people see that they only need to do a few things well. |
| Leading stakeholders to perceive they have powerful systems of support | In some schools, leaders articulate what personnel are expected to do and then assume people will do it well. Support is often short term with minimal opportunity for personnel to try approaches and receive helpful feedback. Sometimes, personnel are reluctant to invest effort, because they feel support is insufficient. | When stakeholders believe they have a quality and quantity of support they need to get their students to excel, they will be much more eager to try to engage in improvement efforts. |
| Leading personnel to experience individual and collective efficacy | In order to accomplish anything, leadership teams must create time for teams to work together to improve learning results. Dedicated, regular, well-planned meeting time and learning time is essential. Time must be organized to ensure that each experience is likely to result in personnel feeling like they will be more effective in ensuring the success of their students. | When the quality of collaboration time improves so that personnel see the immediate benefit to themselves and their students, teams will find ways to increase their collaboration time, and the sense of collective efficacy will grow. |
| Continuously monitoring implementation to improve efforts and outcomes | It is far too easy to raise an issue, address it through a limited action, and move to the next concern. Effective leadership teams continuously look for evidence that their actions result in improved implementation. As well, they look for evidence that improved implementation results in improved outcomes for all student groups. | When leadership teams continuously monitor implementation, they minimize episodic, band-aid approaches and help everyone focus on the critical issues (especially the six gears) that will drive improved learning for all student groups. |

# An Effective Leadership Team: What It Is and What It Isn't

### (X) What It Isn't: Hoping to Create the Perfect Leadership Team While Waiting for the Perfect Team Members

Sometimes, it is easy to see reasons someone might not be an ideal school leadership team member. In fact, some leaders delay the start of leadership team activities, while others avoid launching leadership teams entirely, because they are concerned about who might be willing to serve, who might want to be considered, or who might be the popular choice among their colleagues. Generally, hoping for perfect candidates is not a useful strategy.

### (✓) What It Is: Starting With the Best Team Available and Building Their Capacity to Lead

School leaders take a variety of approaches to developing leadership teams. Some will spend time talking with all school personnel about the qualities of effective school leadership teams. Often, leaders will emphasize the importance of having team members who believe all students have the potential to excel, as long as the school provides the right supports. Often, leaders will emphasize the need to have team members who are excellent listeners and dedicated communicators who are willing to spend time listening to the perspectives of stakeholders (including students, parents, and school personnel), sharing those perspectives with the leadership team, and reporting back to stakeholders in ways that build trust and understanding. As well, leaders will emphasize the importance of having team members who are creative and determined enough to help conceptualize new routines, schedules, practices, procedures, and policies that will build everyone's capacity to contribute in ways that lead to strong academic outcomes for all students. Nonetheless, such processes are not likely to yield a perfect team because there is no such thing. In fact, leaders know that great leadership teams are developed over time. Teams become effective as a result of excellent on-the-job training and learning experiences. Leaders recognize that every school leadership meeting is an opportunity to strengthen the team in a way that will help the team drive the success of all student groups.

## ⓧ What It Isn't: Focusing the Leadership Team on Maintaining Existing Programs, Practices, and Policies

It is essential for school leadership teams to find ways to acknowledge and celebrate both small and large successes. Often, missed opportunities to recognize successes feed a negative culture that magnifies a sense of hopelessness and despair. On the other hand, some leadership teams avoid grappling with the lack of success experienced by some students. Instead of protecting "the way we've always done it," outstanding leadership teams are constantly looking for opportunities to improve in ways that will lead more students to greater levels of success.

## ✓ What It Is: Challenging the Leadership Team to Create a Path to High Levels of Academic Success for All Student Groups

While outstanding leadership teams spend considerable time and energy identifying and celebrating evidence of improvement and success, they also spend considerable time and energy asking hard questions about what might be needed to help more students experience such improvements and successes. They ask, "What supports do other teachers need to help other students achieve similar successes? How can we learn more about the classrooms in our school where students from this particular group are achieving at high levels? Are there other schools, with students like our students, who are achieving better results? If so, what happens at those schools that has influenced their success? How can we help our teachers and support staff feel like they have all the support they need in order to achieve similar results?" Even when schools improve in ways that make them award-winning schools, leadership teams continue to search for new opportunities to refine practices and improve in ways that will generate more successes for more students.

### ❌ What It Isn't: Building the Leadership Team's Understanding of the Rationale Behind the Decisions of Administrators

Some administrators spend a considerable amount of time helping the leadership team understand the dilemmas they face and the constraints that make many decisions difficult. Such dialogue can be important in improving communication and building trust throughout a school. Sometimes, however, the communication is unidirectional: from administrators to the rest of the leadership team. Instead of building trust, unidirectional patterns of communication can quickly erode trust and cause stakeholders to stop listening to administrators and maybe even stop participating in leadership team efforts.

### ✓ What It Is: Building Systems for Engaging the Leadership Team in Facilitating Excellent Multi-Directional Communication Among All Stakeholders

Effective leadership teams assume responsibility for facilitating excellent multi-directional communication. Team members understand that part of their job is to listen to students, parents, colleagues, and administrators. Leadership team members should listen well enough to hear concerns, fears, challenges, benefits, and joys. As well, leadership team members need to assume responsibility for sharing what they learn in constructive, positive ways that build mutual respect, understanding, and trust.

### ❌ What It Isn't: Focusing the Leadership Team on Issues That Will Address the Concerns of Adult Stakeholders

Effective leadership teams do not ignore the concerns of teachers, support staff, administrators, parents, or other adults at the school. A lack of attention to important adult concerns could detract from efforts to build a positive transformational culture among school personnel. However, teams improve the success of all student groups only when they do not let adult concerns outweigh the issues that influence student success.

### ✓ What It Is: Focusing the Leadership Team on Issues That Will Address the Movement of the Gears That Drive Improvement for All Student Groups

Effective leadership teams dedicate most of their time and energy to issues that will drive improved learning outcomes for all student groups. In particular, they avoid spending time on issues that will result in one group of adults "winning" and another group "losing." Instead, they choose to focus on issues that could help students "win" improved learning outcomes. Especially, they focus on ensuring the movement of the six gears that drive improvement for all student groups.

### ✗ What It Isn't: Engaging the Leadership Team in Identifying School Personnel Who Are Less Effective in Improving Learning Outcomes

In every outstanding school, some personnel are more successful than others in implementing practices that lead to better learning outcomes. Effective leadership teams acknowledge, support, and celebrate personnel who improve learning outcomes for their students. They also find ways to encourage and support personnel who experience difficulty in generating improved outcomes for their students; however, effective leadership teams avoid creating cultures in which school personnel feel blamed or ashamed. Instead, effective leadership teams strive to create a culture in which everyone's positive efforts are supported; everyone feels safe discussing strategies, programs, or practices they perceive as difficult; and everyone feels that the leadership team supports them as they endeavor to improve learning outcomes for their students.

### ✓ What It Is: Engaging the Leadership Team in Building Systems That Will Build the Capacity of School Personnel to Ensure the Success of All Student Groups

Effective leadership teams continuously ask themselves how they can create systems of support that ensure all school personnel are likely to improve learning outcomes for all student groups.

Effective leadership teams continuously refine professional learning opportunities, professional learning communities, teacher observation and feedback strategies, and many other systems in ways that help school personnel improve the movement of each of the gears that drive the success of all student groups so that improved learning outcomes are commonplace throughout the school.

## Tips for Leadership Teams

***How Schools Can Optimize the Effectiveness of Leadership Teams (Remember to Review/Consider These Tips Regularly)***

- Engage leadership team members in soliciting input from various stakeholders (including groups of students, parents, community members, and personnel). Elicit ideas about strategies that could help your school improve student success (especially for groups of students who are not achieving their potential). Usually, it is best to focus inquiry on one issue at a time. Ensure that those who provide input know their perspectives are valued and appreciated.
- Create ways to communicate important findings to all stakeholders (without breaking trust or building conflict). Focus upon what has been learned from stakeholders, especially related to how the six gears move or don't move.
- Establish regular, frequent, quality time for leadership team meetings. Also, establish regular, frequent, quality time for team members to meet with the groups they represent. This time is one of the school's most important investments.
- At leadership team meetings, expect team members to report what they learned from their stakeholders, as well as what they communicated to their stakeholders. When leadership team members convene the groups they represent, expect these meetings to include time for the leadership team representative to share issues and concerns discussed and decisions made at leadership team meetings. In addition, meetings should include time for group members to share their understandings

and concerns. Develop high-quality meeting agendas for leadership team members to model and employ.

- Arrange time for building the capacity of leadership team members to assume their roles well. Especially, support leadership team members in learning how to conduct empathy interviews, lead focus groups to acquire stakeholder input, support colleagues in selecting and understanding critical academic concepts and skills, and lead colleagues in collaboratively planning engaging lessons to teach critical academic concepts and skills in ways that will lead to mastery.

- Arrange time for leadership team members to learn about schools where all student groups excel. If possible, arrange opportunities for leadership team members to conduct an in-person school visit. If an in-person visit is not practical, arrange an opportunity for a virtual visit (through Zoom or similar technology) with leadership team members from a school where all student groups excel.

## Where Is Your School on the Road to Developing an Effective Leadership Team?

The school leadership team should consider using the rubric in Table 2.2 to assess the school's progress toward developing an effective leadership team. By reviewing the rubric each semester, the leadership team may identify and celebrate areas of growth and identify areas where additional growth is needed.

Effective Leadership Teams

Table 2.2 Rubric for Assessing Progress Developing an Effective Leadership Team

| | Blazing New Paths of Equity/Excellence (Exemplary) | Entering a Whole New Environment (Approaching) | At Early Mile Markers (Developing) | At the Highway On-Ramp (Waiting) |
|---|---|---|---|---|
| **Stakeholders Believe Leaders Listen to Them** | Even when there is substantial evidence that all student groups excel, leadership team members listen to even more intently to find ways to improve outcomes. | Stakeholders know that leadership team members regularly and sincerely listen to their perspectives and respond accordingly. All stakeholder groups trust that school leaders value them. | Stakeholders perceive that leadership team members making initial efforts to listen to their perspectives and respond accordingly. | Stakeholders don't perceive that anyone listens to their ideas about what needs to happen to improve learning outcomes. |
| **Stakeholders Believe Leadership Decisions Are Student Focused** | Even when there is substantial evidence that all student groups excel, stakeholders commit to pursuing even greater outcomes for students. | Stakeholders believe that most school decisions/actions are designed to help all student groups excel. Stakeholders see evidence that leadership team decisions and actions are making a positive difference for students. | Stakeholders see the leadership team starting to examine/change practices to identify improvement options that will lead to better student outcomes. | Stakeholders don't perceive that anyone examines or challenges the connection between school practices and decisions and student outcomes. |

(Continued)

Table 2.2 (Continued)

| | Blazing New Paths of Equity/Excellence (Exemplary) | Entering a Whole New Environment (Approaching) | At Early Mile Markers (Developing) | At the Highway On-Ramp (Waiting) |
|---|---|---|---|---|
| Stakeholders Understand and Embrace Their Roles in Influencing Improved Learning Outcomes | Even when there is substantial evidence that all student groups excel, stakeholders feel inspired to consider how they can refine their roles to further improve student outcomes. | Stakeholders hold clear, common understandings about their roles in advancing the gears that drive success for all student groups. They embrace those roles collaboratively as they help each other improve individually and collectively. | Stakeholders are beginning to see how they can play a part in moving each of the gears that drive success for all student groups. | Stakeholders don't know how they can be expected to influence improved learning outcomes. Often, stakeholders feel like they're set up to fail. |
| Stakeholders Believe They Have Outstanding Support to Help Them Pursue Their Roles | Even when there is substantial evidence that all student groups excel, stakeholders perceive that their leaders continuously look for ways to improve support. | Stakeholders believe their capacity to improve learning outcomes has improved substantially because of the regular, intensive supports provided by leaders. | Stakeholders are beginning to experience some regular, well-planned, job-embedded supports designed to help them improve outcomes. | Stakeholders feel leaders judge them when they don't improve learning outcomes, but leaders don't feel responsible for helping them improve outcomes. |

(Continued)

Table 2.2 (Continued)

| | Blazing New Paths of Equity/Excellence (Exemplary) | Entering a Whole New Environment (Approaching) | At Early Mile Markers (Developing) | At the Highway On-Ramp (Waiting) |
|---|---|---|---|---|
| Stakeholders Feel Both Individual and Collective Efficacy | Even when there is substantial evidence that all student groups excel, stakeholders continuously look for opportunities to support their colleagues in improving services to students. | Stakeholders believe they have a high likelihood of generating improved learning outcomes for their students because they belong to a capable, professional team that is committed to helping them succeed. | In a no-blame environment, stakeholders experience new structures that provide them real opportunities to learn and practice approaches more likely to lead to improved student outcomes. | Stakeholders often feel isolated and alone. They don't believe the school is likely to achieve improved learning outcomes for students. |
| Stakeholders Believe the School Is Improving Continuously | Even when outcomes are outstanding, the leadership team keeps looking for ways to improve. Stakeholders are proud to "take ownership" of goals most schools would consider impossible to achieve. | Stakeholders see regular evidence that the school leadership team is highlighting and learning from both implementation data and outcome data. Stakeholders see a "snowball effect" as small improvements have rolled into large gains for students. | Stakeholders see the leadership team trying to learn from initial efforts to improve the movement of each of "the gears that drive student success." Stakeholders see these initial efforts as constructive and positive. | Stakeholders almost never hear about improved outcomes, especially for some student groups. Many stakeholders assume that progress is unlikely. |

# References

Aronson, J. (2008). Knowing students as individuals. In M. Pollock (Ed.), *Everyday antiracism: Getting real about race in school* (pp. 67–69). The New Press.

Bandura, A. (2000). Exercise of human agency through collective efficacy. *Current Directions in Psychological Science, 9*(3), 75–78. doi: 10.1111/1467-8721.00064

Chenoweth, K. (2009). *How it's being done: Urgent lessons from unexpected schools.* Harvard Education Press.

Edmonds, R. (1979). Effective schools for the urban poor. *Educational Leadership, 37*(1), 15–18, 20–24.

Goddard, R. D., Hoy, W. K., & Hoy, A. W. (2000). Collective teacher efficacy: Its meaning, measure, and effect on student achievement. *American Education Research Journal, 37*(2), 479–507.

Hattie, J. (2023). *Visible learning, the sequel: A synthesis of over 2,100 meta-analyses relating to achievement.* Routledge.

Johnson, J. F., Uline, C. L., & Munro, S. J. (2023). *When Black students excel: How schools can engage and empower Black students.* New York: Routledge and Taylor & Francis Group.

Johnson, J. F., Uline, C. L., & Perez, L. G. (2017). *Leadership in America's best urban schools.* New York: Routledge and Taylor & Francis Group.

Leithwood, K., Louis, K. S., Anderson, S., & Wahlstrom, K. (2004). *Review of research: How leadership influences student learning.* The Wallace Foundation.

Lezotte, L. W., & Snyder, K. M. (2011). *What effective schools do: Re-envisioning the correlates.* Solution Tree Press.

Marzano, R. J., Waters, T., & McNulty, B. A. (2005). *School leadership that works: From research to results.* Association for Supervision and Curriculum Development.

Robinson, V. (2011). *Student-centered leadership.* San Francisco, CA: Jossey-Bass.

# 3 Positive Transformational Culture

> **Voices of Students and Parents From America's Best Schools**
>
> "This is a second home because I feel so comfortable with my friends and the staff here."
> — Marisa, fourth-grade student,
> Paredes Elementary, Brownsville, TX
>
> "I think the teachers work hard to make us feel connected. You just feel it here. You know you're accepted. It makes you want to be here. It makes you want to try your hardest."
> — Rodrigo, tenth-grade student, Gahr High School, Cerritos, CA
>
> "You can tell when teachers really want you to succeed. They don't just say nice things. They actually work to help make sure you work and learn."
> — Teresa, fifth-grade student, Paredes Elementary School,
> Brownsville, TX

## VIGNETTE E: Dr. Americo Parades Elementary School, Brownsville Independent School District, Brownsville, Texas

**WON NCUST'S AMERICA'S BEST SCHOOL AWARD IN 2017 AND 2024**

*"Ultimately, it's the trust we share amongst each other, because if there's no trust, there's no unity. That's what makes us successful."* These words

articulated by one educator at Paredes Elementary in Brownsville, Texas, were echoed by many.

Paredes educators insisted that the culture they shared at work was dramatically different than the culture of many schools. For example, one teacher emphasized, "It's like a family. It's coming to work, being happy, feeling comfortable with your colleagues and feeling respected by your administrators." Another teacher added, "I think we have a very strong support system. Everyone's always willing to help each other. Whatever situation may arise, I always feel comfortable going to any of the teachers to ask for any sort of help or advice or anything." One teacher explained, "If you love your profession, it's not so much work. It is a part of your life and it's what makes you who you are."

Paredes educators were energized by being part of a talented, committed team of professionals. They seem eager to do whatever they can to help their school succeed because they feel accepted and valued as part of the Paredes team. For example, teachers described how general education and special education teachers work together to get to know their students and co-plan for student success throughout the school year. Similarly, teachers described how they had acquired many of their most useful teaching strategies and approaches because their colleagues were willing to share their best practices.

As the Paredes leadership team builds and sustains a positive, supportive culture for the school's educators, they strive to create a similarly supportive culture for the students. "It's the kids who make the campus," one teacher explained. Another added, "[We help the students] fall in love with learning." Teachers explained that their students fell in love with learning as they came to feel valued, appreciated, and loved by the teachers. Teachers supported each other in creating learning environments where each student was likely to experience a level of support and a quality of attention that would result in them loving school and loving learning.

## VIGNETTE F: Richard Gahr High School, ABC Unified School District, Cerritos, California

### WON NCUST'S AMERICA'S BEST SCHOOL AWARD IN 2024

In a high school where 94 percent of the 1,600 students identify themselves as either Latino/Hispanic, Black/African American, Asian, Filipino, or multi-racial, one might not anticipate seeing students who choose to spend their free time with teachers. However, at Gahr High School, in Los Angeles County, teachers and administrators have worked together to create a culture where all students feel valued and respected by school personnel. The culture is a cornerstone of Gahr's success as a school where few students are suspended or expelled, and every demographic group outperforms the statewide percentage of high school students who meet or exceed state standards.

Everyday instructional routines have influenced the positive culture at Gahr. For example, almost all Gahr teachers are accustomed to posting an objective to help students know what they need to learn concerning each day's lesson. This simple routine makes it easier for students to feel that their teachers want them to succeed. Additionally, Gahr teachers work together to design lessons that are likely to help all their students achieve the daily objective. In particular, teachers have endeavored to design lessons that help students see the relationship between their backgrounds, prior knowledge, and cultures and the concepts and skills students need to learn.

Additionally, non-instructional routines have positively influenced Gahr's culture. For example, contractual agreements helped establish break time and lunchtime routines where teachers remain in their classrooms with their doors open, and students are invited inside to eat with their teachers. While some students choose to eat outside, many students are eager to come into classrooms and interact with school personnel. Students and teachers enjoy the opportunity to get to know each other outside of instructional times.

The informal time to build relationships has resulted in Gahr teachers receiving invitations to students' family events, sporting events, and other activities. Teachers have enjoyed building long-lasting relationships with their students and their students' families that sometimes persist long after students graduate. At Gahr High School, an art pathway produced by students proclaims, "We belong." The simple declaration helps explain why the school achieves remarkable learning outcomes for all student groups.

While educators who visit NCUST award-winning schools notice evidence of all six gears that drive success for all students groups, visitors are most impressed by the culture they see students, parents, and school personnel developing, enjoying, and sustaining. Sometimes, visitors are so mesmerized by the positive transformational culture, they fail to notice the movement of other important gears at America's Best Schools. Both Paredes Elementary (Vignette E) and Gahr High School (Vignette F) offer powerful examples of positive transformational cultures. This chapter will explain what a positive transformational culture is, and it will also clarify why building positive transformational cultures can be difficult and sometimes frustrating, even though the rewards can be substantial.

A positive transformational culture is far more than a culture that welcomes students or expresses kindness. It is far more than a culture that invites students to belong. It is a culture that leads students to believe their success is likely, because they are the institution's chief priority. It is a culture in which students, who may have previously encountered a lack of safety, acceptance, kindness, belonging, or success, transform how they see who they are and all they have the potential to become (Johnson, Uline, & Perez, 2017).

In the absence of a positive transformational culture at school, some students will thrive because they have learned from their parents, other family members, or prior educational experiences that their success is likely. In contrast, however, in the absence of a school-wide positive transformational culture, many students of color, students from low-income communities, students who are emerging as bilingual, students with disabilities, and many other students will struggle. These students may have concluded that their success in school and their success in life is not likely, is not expected, and is not a priority of the institution they attend or the individuals who work within the institution. The accuracy of the students' conclusion is of little consequence. What matters is how the students see themselves and how they see their chances for success.

In Figure 1.1, a positive transformational culture holds a central place within the gear structure. If a positive transformational culture does not exist, the other gears are far less likely to move. In the absence of a positive transformational culture, many students will be less likely to invest the effort to try, persist, and excel, especially if they do not have the benefit of prior experiences that convince them that their effort is likely to be rewarded with success. As Johnson, Uline, and Perez (2019) explained, "Without a positive transformational culture, other improvement efforts are built on quicksand" (p. 141).

## What Leadership Teams Accomplish Through Positive Transformational Cultures

After visiting classrooms in an NCUST award-winning school, one teacher argued, "I could get kids to learn to read, think, and write like the students in these classes, if my students were more like their students." Although her students shared many of the same demographic characteristics as the students in the classroom she observed, she commented that her students didn't try to think deeply about what they were reading. She said, "My kids don't want to think at all. They don't want to try."

In truth, the teacher who was complaining about her students taught some students who were thriving academically and achieving impressive successes. In every school, one can find some remarkable students who have been inspired to try, persist, and excel. Unfortunately, in struggling schools, many more students are convinced that their behavioral and/or academic success is unlikely or impossible. While some students are reluctant to engage because they fear negative responses from their teachers, others are more fearful of teasing, bullying, or other negative behavior from their classmates. Some students have responded to their frustrations by rebelling against the system they believe has doomed them to fail. Others try to reduce their risk of failure by minimizing the likelihood that teachers or classmates notice them at all. Sometimes, in spite of the good efforts of educators, students who perceive themselves as unlikely to succeed refuse to try and, consequently, deny themselves the opportunity to excel. What students believe their teachers think of them influences students' engagement. What students believe their classmates think of them influences students' engagement.

In the schools NCUST has awarded, we have found students who share many similarities with students in struggling schools: sometimes schools in the same districts, the same neighborhoods, with the same funding, with the same demographics. Often, the award-winning schools have many students who experienced academic frustration in prior grade levels or in prior schools, whose families primarily speak a language other than English, or whose parents achieved minimal successes in school. Nonetheless, in NCUST award-winning schools, the overwhelming majority of students seem convinced that they can succeed academically, learn challenging concepts and skills, be leaders in their school and in their communities, and successfully pursue their aspirations. In large part, students have reached these powerful conclusions about their capacity to succeed because of the positive transformational culture established throughout their schools.

In schools where all student groups excel, students are likely to experience a culture that positively transforms how they perceive themselves as learners, thinkers, scholars, citizens, problem-solvers, and leaders. Whatever advantages or challenges students have experienced at home or in prior schooling, the positive transformational culture convinces students they are valuable and valued, worthy of respect and respected, lovable and loved, capable of academic success and successful.

In schools where all student groups excel, leadership teams have developed a school-wide culture (in classrooms and outside of classrooms) that leads students from all demographic groups to see themselves as worthwhile individuals, capable scholars, productive citizens, and ethical leaders. To develop such a culture, leadership teams first work to ensure that all students experience school as a place where they are safe, both physically and emotionally.

## *Leadership Teams Worked With All Stakeholders to Lead Students to Feel Physically and Emotionally Safe*

Students are far less likely to focus their energies on academic tasks if they are fearful about negative responses from teachers or other students. Frequently, students in struggling schools report fear of being teased, bullied, or assaulted by peers because of issues related to race, gender, gender identity, language background, accents, disabilities, perceived intelligence, or other physical characteristics (such as body size, hair, or skin pigmentation). Compared to students in NCUST award-winning schools, students in struggling schools are far more likely to report fearing humiliation or angry responses from their teachers when they answer questions incorrectly. As well, in NCUST award-winning schools, students are much less likely to report concerns about their physical or emotional safety than students in struggling schools, even though school demographics might be similar. As one student from award-winning Maplewood Richmond Heights High School in St. Louis, Missouri, explained, "There's not nearly as much drama here as you find in other high schools. We feel accepted for who we are, regardless of race, academics, or sexual orientation. Teachers accept us and we accept each other" (Johnson, Uline, & Munro, 2023, p. 27).

Often teacher leaders and administrators in NCUST award-winning schools reported that establishing a safe environment for everyone was an important first step in changing the culture of the school. In many outstanding schools, this meant that all school personnel committed to addressing (not ignoring) situations that led students to feel physically or emotionally unsafe. In contrast, when NCUST personnel have interviewed students in struggling schools, students are more likely to share that when they tell school personnel they are teased, bullied, or assaulted, some adults fail to act.

In highly successful schools, like Parades Elementary (Vignette E) and Gahr High School (Vignette F), students indicated that they rarely experienced problems with other students. Leadership teams promoted a culture that emphasized making everyone feel safe and comfortable. When behavior occurred that made students feel unsafe, educators used those situations as opportunities to teach students about the harmful impact on individuals and on the larger culture the school wanted to create for everyone. For example, at Young Men's Leadership Academy (Vignette B), teachers, administrators, and students led many discussions about how negative behavior influenced the culture of brotherhood at the all-boys school.

Additionally, it is important to note that at many NCUST award-winning schools, leadership teams established and reinforced routines through which they regularly acknowledged and celebrated positive student behavior that strengthened the desired school-wide safe culture. In schools like Concourse Village Elementary (currently named Leaders of Excellence, Advocacy, and Discovery – LEAD) in New York City's Bronx and Wynnebrook Elementary in West Palm Beach, Florida, teachers and administrators spent considerable time and energy acknowledging students who modeled the school's core values and handled potentially difficult situations in ways that promoted a safe, welcoming culture (Johnson et al., 2023).

## *Leadership Teams Worked With All Stakeholders to Lead Students to Feel Valued, Respected, and Loved*

In many high-performing schools, safety was a first consideration in creating a positive transformational culture; however, much more needed to change to transform how students perceived themselves. Outstanding leadership teams recognized that, even though the great majority of educators care sincerely for their students, some students may assume they are neither valued, respected, nor loved by school personnel. Before their first school day, some students may assume the worst about their teachers, administrators, and other school personnel. Some students may have attended a school for years, yet feel as if they are trespassers in a school meant for "other people's children" (Delpit, 1995). Beyond creating a safe culture, leadership teams sought to create a culture in which all students believed their happiness and success were important priorities.

In NCUST award-winning schools, overwhelmingly students reported that school personnel cared about them, their families, their academic success, and their success in life. Noddings (2012) emphasized the importance of caring in helping children learn. In America's Best Schools, students from all demographic groups were convinced that educators cared enough about them to get to know them, to know their strengths, interests, and needs; to know their families; and to use the information acquired to make whatever adjustments were necessary to facilitate their success (Johnson et al., 2019).

To create cultures in which all student groups felt valued, respected, and loved, leadership teams created deliberate opportunities for teachers and other school personnel to get to know each other. For example, at Gahr High School (Vignette F), teachers chose to open their classrooms to students at snack and lunch times so they could have opportunities to build relationships with students. With the same goal of improving teacher-student relationships, at O'Farrell Charter High School in San Diego, California, leaders created a home base program that helped each student build a four-year relationship with one teacher who served as a support and advocate (Johnson et al., 2023).

In schools that did not alter schedules to provide greater time for relationship building, leaders helped teachers feel comfortable using small amounts of instructional time in ways that could enhance relationship building. For example, at Veterans Memorial Early College High School (Vignette C), students expressed appreciation for the way teachers used small amounts of classroom time to acknowledge their participation in recent athletic events, express concern about ill family members, or inquire about student participation in other extra-curricular activities. Similarly, at Young Men's Leadership Academy (Vignette B), students shared that teachers found small ways to get to know students and help them feel like members of a community. Principal White explained that a core principle of YMLA's success was articulated by author and speaker Josh McDowell, who said, "Rules without relationships lead to rebellion" (see https://www.josh.org/ddl-video/rules-without-relationships-lead-to-rebellion/).

In addition to promoting opportunities for teachers to get to know students, many leaders of NCUST award-winning schools promoted opportunities for school personnel to get to know the families of their students. Leaders recognized that some teachers might have minimal knowledge of, or experience with, families from the racial, ethnic, linguistic, or socio-economic backgrounds that were common at their school. They recognized that teachers might have misconceptions about families and those misconceptions could result in poor communication and missed opportunities to build trusting relationships. As a result, leadership teams took time to support teachers in learning about the families they served. As well, leadership teams created opportunities for teachers to engage positively with parents and other family members.

By strengthening relationships, educators increased the likelihood that students believed that adults at school knew them, cared about them, and wanted them to succeed in school and in life. Cornelius-White (2007) found that the impact of teacher–student relationships has been demonstrated in over 119 studies, with an effect size of 0.72 (more powerful than student's prior achievement, teacher professional development, student's home environment, phonics instruction, student's socioeconomic status, class management, and many other factors).

In NCUST award-winning schools, leaders worked to strengthen relationships with all students, including students who were least likely to have enjoyed positive relationships with school personnel. While the power of teacher–student relationships is important for all students, Ferguson (2008) found that teacher–student relationships have an even greater impact on the effort of Black/African American students and Latino/Hispanic students.

## *Leadership Teams Worked With All Stakeholders to Lead Students to Feel Capable and Successful*

To ensure that the school culture truly transformed how students perceived themselves, administrators and teacher leaders in NCUST award-winning schools worked to help their colleagues lead all students to feel academically capable and successful. As in many NCUST award-winning schools, teachers at Gahr High School (Vignette F) committed to posting clear statements about what students were expected to learn as a result of each lesson. Teachers broke apart complex standards and helped students see how each day's lesson would help students develop mastery of important academic concepts. Teachers helped students know what they needed to focus upon to bolster their school success.

At Paredes Elementary (Vignette E), Gahr High School (Vignette F), and many other NCUST award-winning schools, teachers supported each other in creating lessons that helped students see how lessons connected with their backgrounds, interests, cultures, and prior knowledge. Teachers made difficult concepts seem less foreign and more familiar to students.

Also, at many NCUST award-winning schools, teachers revised grading policies to encourage students to make multiple efforts to demonstrate their understanding of important concepts and skills. Teachers helped students feel good about the progress they were making in learning rigorous skills that represented grade-level skills or beyond. By doing so, teachers encouraged students to work hard and persist.

Ultimately, in NCUST award-winning schools, the positive transformational culture led many students to transform their perceptions of their ability to meet the behavioral and academic expectations of their teachers and administrators; to assume leadership roles in their classroom, school, and community; and to interact as thoughtful, engaged scholars who could access and use information to solve real problems. Students from all racial, linguistic, and economic backgrounds, regardless of prior behavioral or academic success, changed how they perceived themselves and their chances of success in school and in life.

## *Leadership Teams Led School Personnel to Feel Valued and Capable as Members of a Powerful School-Wide Team*

Schools that establish a positive transformational culture for all students also create positive transformational cultures for the adults who work there. In highly effective schools, we found leadership teams working together to create a culture that transformed how all school personnel perceived their chances of professional success.

To create a culture in which school personnel felt valued and capable, leaders prioritized the perspectives of school personnel, especially on matters related to instruction. Some school leaders expect teachers to follow a scripted curriculum without question, rely on computer-assisted software (even when there is little evidence of learning success), or follow a district-mandated scope and sequence chart that has never proved successful at ensuring the success of their students. In contrast, administrators and teacher leaders in NCUST award-winning schools listen thoughtfully to the wisdom of school personnel. There is not always agreement about courses of action; however, school personnel are much more likely to feel listened to, respected, and appreciated than educators in typical schools. Teachers at NCUST award-winning schools almost never report feeling blamed; however, they persistently talk about being supported by their colleagues and leaders. While asking for anonymity, one teacher at an NCUST award-winning school explained:

> I've been offered positions at other schools where the kids come from better neighborhoods and have many other advantages, but I politely turn them down, in part because I love my students here, but also because I love being in a place where I'm not treated as an assembly-line worker. Here, they respect me as someone who wants the very best for all my students, who will always look for ways to improve, and who will always work to support my colleagues.

In NCUST award-winning schools, school personnel are much more likely to feel supported by their colleagues, by teacher leaders, and by school administrators. Teacher collaboration occurs frequently (sometimes multiple times a week), because teachers value the opportunity to support each other. At Paredes Elementary (Vignette E), like many other NCUST award-winning schools, teachers emphasized that they had developed and sustained a level of trust among their colleagues and a sense of family that helped them believe, together, they could improve the trajectory of their students' lives.

Both collegial trust and a sense of family were enhanced as school leaders emphasized growth and improvement rather than expecting teachers to exhibit perfection. Often, teachers in NCUST award-winning schools reported they felt supported far more often than they felt they were being evaluated. They perceived that school leaders focused persistently on a few important teaching concepts. As a result, teachers felt they were constantly improving their use of the important teaching concepts. Teachers felt their leaders held high expectations for them; however, they also felt that the expectations were attainable, because the expectations did not change with the weather: expectations were constant over months and even years. Also, teachers believed that expectations were attainable, because teachers benefitted from high-quality support (at times from administrators, often from colleagues, and, when necessary, from outside experts identified by the school leadership team). Leaders held themselves accountable for ensuring that teachers had clear, useful, job-embedded support that would help teachers lead their students to high levels of academic success.

## Why Establishing a Positive Transformational Culture Is Challenging Yet Rewarding

In schools with a positive transformational culture, students who previously thought they were incapable of reading grade-level texts learned they could channel their efforts in ways that ensured their ability to read, comprehend, and learn from complex material. Students who previously believed they were "discipline problems" transformed their perception of themselves and recognized they were well equipped to serve as positive role models, productive citizens, and outstanding leaders in their classrooms, schools, and communities. Students who had never imagined themselves mastering academic concepts transformed their self-images and recognized themselves as bright and creative scholars who could grapple with and solve complex problems and communicate their ideas, questions, and conclusions well.

Similarly, in schools with positive transformational cultures, personnel who previously believed they rarely taught their students anything of value came to see themselves as part of a team that would lead students to impressive accomplishments that far exceeded district or state expectations. Teachers recognized themselves as important collaborators in a coordinated effort to improve the lives of all their students.

Even though the benefits of a positive transformational culture are immense, many students in typical schools experience a culture that reinforces their most negative perceptions of themselves. Often, in the same schools, teachers and other school personnel experience a similarly negative culture. Establishing a positive transformational culture requires deliberate effort over a sustained period of time with substantial support. Table 3.1 describes some of the challenges and rewards of establishing a positive transformational culture.

Table 3.1 Challenges and Rewards of Establishing a Positive Transformational Culture

| Issue | The Challenges | The Rewards |
|---|---|---|
| **Leading students to feel physically and emotionally safe** | A lack of school-wide consistency can erode the sense of safety at a school. If some staff feel that it isn't their job or they don't have the time to reinforce safety issues, the inconsistencies will impede the development of a positive culture. *All* school personnel must assume responsibility for reporting and addressing issues that threaten safety. | If all adults actively assume responsibility for addressing safety issues, students will learn quickly that the school prioritizes their safety. |
| **Leading students to feel physically and emotionally safe** | A lack of school-wide consistency in the ways school personnel interact with students can erode or destroy the school's positive transformational culture. All school personnel need to monitor how they interact with students to ensure that they consistently model respectful interactions. Some school personnel may need support in changing their ways of interacting with students in difficult situations. | By expecting personnel to model positive interactions and by providing personnel the support they need, a positive school-wide culture will develop more quickly. |
| **Leading students to feel physically and emotionally safe** | School personnel may need training and/or modeling to lead conversations that help students learn from situations that resulted in others experiencing physical or emotional harm. | Training personnel to lead constructive conversations will reduce the emphasis on punishment and promote social learning. |

(Continued)

Table 3.1 (Continued)

| Issue | The Challenges | The Rewards |
|---|---|---|
| **Leading students to feel valued, respected, and loved** | Teachers may feel that they don't have time to get to know students or help students feel valued. Leadership teams may need to consider options for modifying schedules or encouraging teachers to use some instructional time for relationship building. | Small, regular amounts of time devoted to relationship building can accelerate learning, especially for students who have been disengaged. |
| **Leading students to feel valued, respected, and loved** | Teachers may feel uncomfortable or even fearful about interacting with the parents of their students. Teachers may have misconceptions about parents that might prevent constructive relationships. Training, modeling, and support can help teachers interact successfully with parents. | By helping teachers know how to interact constructively with parents and by supporting teachers in getting to know parents, the school can quickly help students and families feel valued. |
| **Leading students to feel valued, respected, and loved** | The development of relationships takes time. Leadership teams should consider engaging students in empathy interviews to learn more about classroom/school practices that increase and decrease the extent to which students feel valued, respected, and loved. | By listening to the concerns and insights of students, leadership teams can identify opportunities to support teachers in helping students feel valued, respected, and loved. |
| **Leading students to feel capable and successful** | Some teachers try to get students to feel more capable by teaching them easier concepts/skills. Often, those efforts fail. Teachers may need support in designing lessons that lead students to learn grade-level concepts. Regular, focused teacher collaboration may be the best way to provide such support; however, effective collaboration requires both time and trust. | By structuring time for collaboration and building trust among teacher teams, teachers will develop lessons that help students perceive that they can learn challenging concepts and skills. |

(Continued)

Positive Transformational Culture

Table 3.1 (Continued)

| Issue | The Challenges | The Rewards |
|---|---|---|
| Leading school personnel to feel valued and capable | Often, schools handcuff teachers to processes and routines. It is important for leaders to find ways to allow teachers to be accountable for learning results by maximizing their decision-making power concerning teaching processes. For teachers who have not enjoyed flexibility with accountability, they may require substantial support. | When teachers understand that they are allowed (and even expected) to think, problem solve, and be creative about how they can help their students master challenging concepts, often the outcomes will exceed expectations. |
| Leading school personnel to feel valued and capable | Often teachers aren't sure what to focus upon to help them improve learning results for their students. The uncertainty is often due to the district's lack of focus or ever-changing focus. School personnel need consistent focus and consistent high-quality support so that they continuously improve their professional practice. | Teams of teachers who know specifically what they are endeavoring to improve about their teaching, who know that the focus is not likely to change until they demonstrate mastery, and who know they have high-quality job-embedded support will advance quickly toward teacher collective efficacy, as described in Chapter 2. |

# A Positive Transformational Culture: What It Is and What It Isn't

**(X) What It Isn't: Charging a Few Administrators and/or Teachers With the Responsibility of Ensuring That All Students Are Physically and Emotionally Safe**

> If students perceive that some school personnel (i.e. some teachers, paraprofessionals, custodial staff) will not enforce expectations related to physical or emotional safety, a lack of safety may persist. If students find inconsistencies in expectations, misbehavior could escalate and the school culture could deteriorate.

**(✓) What It Is: Developing a Shared Responsibility for Ensuring All Students are Physically and Emotionally Safe**

> In NCUST award-winning schools, all personnel (even part-time staff), share a commitment to ensuring the physical and emotional safety of all students. One parent explained, "The adults at this school protect all the children as if they are protecting their own kids." Educators take pride in their efforts to minimize the number of incidents that threaten safety.

**(X) What It Isn't: Ignoring the Ways in Which the Comments of Some Personnel Lead Students to Feel Unsafe**

> In some schools, leaders talk about the importance of treating all students with respect; however, problematic incidents are ignored. For example, in struggling schools, there are times when student misbehavior was triggered by insensitive comments made by school personnel. Students are held accountable for their misbehavior, but leaders lack the will to address the adult behavior that precipitated the incident. In struggling schools, most students can accurately identify which personnel are most likely to make comments that belittle them, embarrass them, or make them feel emotionally vulnerable.

## ✓ What It Is: Supporting All Personnel in Modeling Behavior That Makes All Students Feel Valued and Respected. Expecting Personnel to Treat Every Student as One of the School's Most Important Clients

Many leaders in NCUST award-winning schools have shared their strong expectation that school personnel model concern and respect for all students, even in difficult situations. This expectation comes not only from administrators but also from teacher leaders who recognize that when a teacher treats a student poorly during period 4, it negatively influences the student's behavior when they arrive at their class for period 5. It is important to note, however, that administrators and teachers work to support teachers in modifying how they handle difficult situations. Often, in NCUST award-winning schools, colleagues model exemplary ways of making students feel valued and respected during difficult situations.

## ✗ What It Isn't: Insisting That Every Minute Be Devoted to Teaching Academic Content

The thrust to improve test scores has led some school leaders to insist that every minute be spent on academic content. Generally, however, data from those schools reveal minimal gains, at best. While it is important to ensure adequate time for instruction, the push for instructional time can be counterproductive if it diminishes attention to the needs of the students we seek to instruct.

## ✓ What It Is: Dedicating Time to Ensure All Students Feel Valued, Respected, and Loved

When possible, effective leadership teams structure time in ways that give teachers and students opportunities to get to know each other and build positive relationships. Leaders help teachers understand that attending to students social and emotional needs on a regular and timely basis can enhance the effectiveness of instructional efforts. In NCUST award-winning schools, educators continuously seek to learn from their students about the practices that increase and decrease the extent to which students feel valued, respected, and loved.

### ❌ What It Isn't: Teaching Students Easier Concepts to Make Them Feel Successful

>When students are asked to learn concepts/skills considered appropriate for lower grade levels, students may assume their teachers don't believe they can learn grade-level concepts and skills. Many students will resent such approaches and refuse to engage in instruction.

### ✓ What It Is: Teaching Students Grade-Level Concepts and Skills

>In NCUST award-winning schools, students know they are being challenged to learn grade-level concepts and skills. As well, students believe they are receiving abundant support to help them learn grade-level concepts and skills well. Students see themselves developing deeper understanding. They are proud of all they have learned, and they look forward to learning more.

### ❌ What It Isn't: Sidestepping the Difficulty of Supporting Teachers in Learning How to Teach Grade-Level Concepts and Skills to Students Who Previously Have Experienced Minimal Learning Success at School

>Teaching students who previously have experienced minimal learning success is hard. Often school and district leaders sidestep the difficulty by expecting teachers to follow "with fidelity" textbooks, workbooks, scripted programs, and computer-assisted programs.

### ✓ What It Is: Building Quality Teacher Collaboration That Helps Teachers Design Lessons That Lead All Student Groups to Learn Challenging Academic Concepts and Skills

>All students groups (including students who previously experienced minimal learning success) are much more likely to learn grade-level concepts and skills when their teachers have

worked together to plan lessons that focus their thinking; build upon their prior knowledge; tap into their interests; and inspire connections to their backgrounds, cultures, and experiences. The pursuit of high-quality teacher collaboration requires a high level of trust among school personnel. Trust is not developed automatically or quickly. It is earned and nurtured over time.

## Tips for Leadership Teams

*How Schools Can Advance a Positive Transformational Culture (Remember to Review and Implement These Tips Regularly)*

- Ensure that all personnel (including teachers, support staff, and part-time staff) know how to respond firmly, consistently, and respectfully to situations that threaten students emotionally or physically. Ensure that everyone understands the importance of building and protecting a culture in which *all* students feel safe at school.

- Engage teachers and other school personnel in organizing and leading regular workshops that help teachers learn respectful ways to respond to difficult situations with students. While minimizing blame, the workshops should encourage everyone to build and protect a culture in which *all* students feel safe at school.

- When administrators learn that school personnel have engaged in behavior that results in some students feeling diminished or unsafe, administrators should discuss the behavior with the responsible individual respectfully, calmly, and with supportive suggestions for handling future situations. The administrator should also, however, ensure that the individual understands the non-negotiable expectation that all students should be treated with dignity and respect, even when students misbehave.

- Engage teachers and other school personnel in organizing and leading workshops that help educators learn how to prevent the escalation of undesirable student behavior by acknowledging and reinforcing positive student behavior that contributes to a positive transformational culture. Encourage teachers to work toward doubling or tripling their recognition of positive student behavior. As well, the workshops should help educators learn how to respond to undesirable student behavior in ways that teach students how to handle difficult situations appropriately and respectfully. The workshops should help school personnel know how to minimize the use of punitive approaches and maximize the use of restorative approaches. When punitive approaches are appropriate and necessary, school personnel should know to use those approaches in ways that help students understand that they are still valued and respected; however, the misbehavior is unacceptable because it damages the culture that the school wants all students to enjoy.

- Engage school personnel in conducting empathy interviews to determine what happens at school that helps them feel valued, respected, and loved. As well, empathy interviews should be used to determine what happens at school that leads students to think they are not valued, respected, and loved. It is important to ensure that students from all groups are included, but especially those groups who experience less academic success and less behavioral success at school. Information learned from the empathy interviews should be shared discreetly among school personnel in ways that lead to specific plans for improving the culture experienced by all student groups.

- Engage the leadership team in examining the school's master calendar to identify possible strategies for dedicating time for relationship building among teachers and students. Additionally, the leadership team should consider ways of encouraging teachers to take short amounts of time to promote relationship building. As well, the leadership team should consider strategies for encouraging and supporting teachers in building relationships with parents.

- Engage the leadership team in examining the school's master calendar to identify regular times for teams of teachers to meet, collaborate, and plan lessons that are more likely to lead all students to feel capable and successful. In addition to scheduling time, the school leadership team should consider how to ensure that the collaboration time will be used in ways that build trust among school personnel and help educators build upon their best practices.

- The school leadership team should carefully examine the curricular tools that teachers are expected to use. Where there is not strong, consistent evidence of academic growth for the school's students, consideration should be given to providing teachers opportunities to modify, supplement, or otherwise change how the curricular tools are used to maximize the academic growth of the school's students. It is important to create a professional culture in which teachers feel that the focus is on improving learning results, not simply implementing a required program.

# Where Is Your School on the Road to Developing a Positive Transformational Culture?

The school leadership team should consider using the rubric in Table 3.2 to assess the school's progress toward developing a positive transformational culture. By reviewing the rubric each semester, the leadership team may identify and celebrate areas of growth and identify areas where additional growth is needed.

Table 3.2 Rubric for Assessing Progress Developing a Positive Transformational Culture

| | Blazing New Paths of Equity/Excellence (Exemplary) | Entering a Whole New Environment (Approaching) | At Early Mile Markers (Developing) | At the Highway On-Ramp (Waiting) |
|---|---|---|---|---|
| Leading students to feel physically and emotionally safe | When there is substantial evidence that all student groups feel physically and emotionally safe, leadership team members listen to students even more intently to find ways to improve safety. | Students (including students from groups that didn't feel safe at school) see clear evidence of improvements that make them feel safer at school. Students see the improvements as evidence that educators care. | Students (including students from groups that don't feel safe at school) perceive that educators are listening to understand the issues that make them feel unsafe. | Some groups of students do not feel physically safe or emotionally safe at school. Both their school attendance and their engagement in learning are low. |
| Leading students to feel valued, respected, and loved | When there is substantial evidence that all student groups feel valued, respected, and loved, leadership team members listen to students even more intently to find ways to increase the likelihood that all students will believe educators care about them. | Students (including students from groups that didn't feel valued, respected, and loved and their parents) see clear evidence of improvements that make them think school personnel care about them. | Students (including students from groups that don't feel valued, respected, and loved and their parents) perceive that educators are listening to understand the issues that make them feel educators don't care about them. | Some groups of students do not feel valued, respected, and loved at school. They think educators don't know or understand them. They are reluctant to exert the effort necessary to succeed because they don't believe educators care. |

(Continued)

Table 3.2 (Continued)

| | Blazing New Paths of Equity/Excellence (Exemplary) | Entering a Whole New Environment (Approaching) | At Early Mile Markers (Developing) | At the Highway On-Ramp (Waiting) |
|---|---|---|---|---|
| **Leading students to feel capable and successful** | Even when there is substantial evidence that all student groups feel capable of achieving grade-level successes, leadership team members listen to students to find ways to increase the likelihood that all students will perceive that educators believe in their capacity to learn challenging content. | Students (including students from groups that didn't feel capable of achieving grade-level successes) see clear evidence of improvements that make them think school personnel believe in their capacity to learn grade-level concepts and skills. | Students (including students from groups that don't feel capable of achieving grade-level successes) perceive that educators are listening to understand the issues that make them feel their academic success is unlikely. | Some groups of students do not feel capable of achieving grade-level successes. They think educators don't believe they are able to succeed. They are reluctant to try to succeed because they don't believe their success is possible. |
| **Leading school personnel to feel valued and capable** | Even when there is substantial evidence that all school personnel feel valued and capable, personnel perceive that school leaders continuously look for ways to improve support. | School personnel (including personnel who did not feel valued or capable) see clear evidence of improvements that make them think school leaders value them and believe in their capacity to play an important role in the school's success. | School personnel (including personnel who do not feel valued or capable) perceive that the school leadership team is listening to understand the issues that make them feel undervalued and unsuccessful. | Some school personnel feel they are not valued. Some feel they are not capable of successfully educating the students they serve. They are reluctant to invest more effort because they doubt that their efforts will be acknowledged, appreciated, or successful. |

# References

Cornelius-White, J. (2007). Learner-centered teacher-student relationships are effective: A meta-analysis. *Review of Educational Research, 77*(1), 113–143.

Delpit, L. (1995). *Other people's children: Cultural conflict in the classroom.* New York: The New Press.

Ferguson, R. F. (2008). *Toward excellence with equity: An emerging vision for closing the achievement gap.* Cambridge, MA: Harvard Education Press.

Johnson, J. F., Uline, C. L., & Munro, S. J. (2023). *When Black students excel: How schools can engage and empower Black students.* New York: Routledge and Taylor & Francis Group.

Johnson, J. F., Uline, C. L., & Perez, L. (2017). *Leadership in America's best urban schools.* New York: Routledge and Taylor & Francis Group.

Johnson, J. F., Uline, C. L., & Perez, L. (2019). *Teaching practices from America's best urban schools: A guide for school and classroom leaders.* New York: Routledge and Taylor & Francis Group.

Noddings, N. (2012). The caring relationship in teaching. *Oxford Review of Education, 38*(6), 771–781.

# 4 | Rigorous Curricula

> **Voices of Students and Parents From America's Best Schools**
>
> "I really liked reading *The Watsons Go to Birmingham* [by Christopher Paul Curtis]. It is historical fiction, but it is based on real things that happened to Black people in the 1960s. I love that we get to read and discuss real books about real issues."
> – Marcus, fifth-grade student at Wynnebrook Elementary, West Palm Beach, Florida
>
> "I have a son here at Stillman and a daughter who attended Stillman but is now in high school. My daughter feels like she was better prepared in math and science than kids who went to other middle schools. The teachers here make sure kids will succeed when they move to high school."
> – A parent of a student at Stillman Middle School, Brownsville, Texas
>
> "Multiplication is a little bit challenging, but when I do it right, it's actually really easy. And it makes sense because you're just adding multiple times."
> – Latisha, third-grade student at Wynnebrook Elementary, West Palm Beach, Florida

## VIGNETTE G: Wynnebrook Elementary, West Palm Beach, Florida

**WON NCUST'S AMERICA'S BEST SCHOOL AWARD IN 2018**

The state of Florida has rated Wynnebrook Elementary in West Palm Beach, Florida, as an "A" school for 19 of the past 21 years. With over 80% of the students meeting free- or reduced-price lunch criteria and almost 90% identifying as Latino/Hispanic or Black/African American, Wynnebrook outperforms many Florida schools in more affluent communities. However, there was a time when learning results were very different.

When Jeff Pegg became principal at Wynnebrook in 1999–2000, few of the school's students were reading at grade level, and many students were performing two or three years below grade level. Wynnebrook students had basal readers; however, very few of the students could read the stories. Principal Pegg asked the teachers if they realized many of their students could not read most of the words in the basal readers they had distributed. The teachers responded, "Of course, we know. They [the students] came to us that way."

The school district's curriculum department endeavored to improve literacy instruction district-wide by developing a scope and sequence that specified when teachers were expected to teach every standard specified by the state, even if the standard had limited value in preparing students to develop strong literacy.

Principal Pegg worked with teacher leaders at the school to develop an approach to teaching literacy that teachers perceived as logical and reasonable. The teachers refined the scope and sequence to focus on the most important literacy standards. Mr. Pegg argued if the district mandates didn't make sense to the teachers, the mandates were not likely to work. Teacher leaders helped select sets of leveled books that allowed teachers to help students advance their reading level. As well, Principal Pegg sent teacher leaders to acquire professional development to help them work as teams to support each other to improve literacy instruction.

In 2016, Principal Pegg was promoted, and Suzanne Berry (a former teacher and assistant principal at Wynnebrook) replaced him, building upon many of the practices they worked together to establish. Instead of attempting to cover all state standards in compliance with a rigid scope and sequence chart, teacher leaders and administrators work together to ensure all Wynnebrook students demonstrate mastery of the most important grade-level concepts and skills. Teachers collaborate regularly to support each other in planning, delivering, and refining lessons that lead students to master important literacy skills. As a result, today, most Wynnebrook students enjoy reading materials at or beyond grade level.

## VIGNETTE H: Stillman Middle School, Brownsville, Texas

### WON NCUST'S AMERICA'S BEST SCHOOL AWARD IN 2024

*Stillman Middle School serves over 1,000 Latino/Hispanic students, of whom two-thirds meet low-income criteria and more than a fourth are emerging as bilingual. Academic rigor prevails throughout this school, located only a few miles from the U.S./Mexico border.*

At Stillman, courses are designed to ensure that when students leave eighth grade, they are achieving or exceeding state standards in reading, mathematics, science, and social studies. Teachers organize courses and lessons to provide students practical, hands-on experiences that build their understanding of academic concepts. One student explained, "The teachers are very hands on. They give us hands-on tasks and we work with each other as a team." Teachers explained how they used data from frequent assessments to determine specifically what students understood, and didn't understand, about important grade-level objectives. Then they used small-group instruction and individual student conferences to address specifically what students needed to learn.

When students have learned middle school content, Stillman teachers provide high-school courses and prepare Stillman students to take the state's end-of-course high school examinations for English I, algebra I, and biology. Teachers continue to support each other in developing hands-on, practical experiences that help students understand the concepts and master the skills most Texas students don't learn until high school. In 2023, 90% of the Stillman middle school students who took the state's end-of-course algebra I test met or exceeded grade-level expectations, compared to 43% of high school students statewide. Similarly, 89% of Stillman Middle School students who took the *end-of-course biology test met or exceeded grade-level expectations, compared to 56% of high school students statewide.*

---

Chapter 3 explained how a positive transformational culture plays a central role in advancing learning and improving lives for all student groups. The gear labeled "positive transformational culture" is at the heart of Figure 1.1, illustrating how improvement of the culture experienced by students and school personnel can accelerate the movement of all the other gears. However, a positive transformational culture alone will not drive the success of all student groups. To maximize student success, the culture must influence the improvement of curricular rigor; the monitoring, confirming, and enhancing of learning; effective initial instruction; and intervention and enrichment (all the other gears). Simultaneously, the movement of the other gears can enhance the improvement of a positive transformational culture.

The rigor of the curricula students experience has a powerful influence on all the gears. Any students who do not have real opportunities to learn rigorous academic concepts and skills are not likely to demonstrate sufficient academic growth and success in school, postsecondary education, careers, or life. A meta-analysis by the American Institutes for Research (AIR) found that rigorous math and reading programs especially benefited Black/African American students, Latino/Hispanic students, and students whose families met low-income criteria, when paired with adequate support (Pane, Griffin, McCaffrey, & Karam, 2015). Similarly, Education Trust (2020) found that students whose families met low-income criteria and students of color suffered greater academic losses when they were denied opportunities to access rigorous curricula, yet their chances of academic success were enhanced when schools provided access to rigorous curricula, complemented by adequate support systems.

## What Leadership Teams Accomplish Through Rigorous Curricula

In many schools, teachers endeavor to cover the entire curriculum for the grade level and the content area they teach. In some schools, this means addressing all state standards. In other schools, it means completing the entire textbook. In others, it might mean teaching all the learning objectives associated with a district-adopted program. Often, school districts will push educators to follow a specific scope and sequence, intended to ensure all state standards and all learning objectives are presented to students. Marzano (2003) argued, however, that covering all the standards may not be "viable." There may not be enough hours in the school day or enough days in the school year for teachers to teach their students all the standards or all the learning objectives.

In contrast, in NCUST's award-winning schools, leaders help teachers resist the temptation (or the mandate) to teach more concepts and skills than can reasonably be learned in a school year. For example, at Wynnebrook Elementary (Vignette G), leaders did not require teachers to follow the district's scope and sequence, which addressed every state literacy standard, at the risk of teaching many standards poorly. Instead, Principal Pegg, and later Principal Berry, engaged teachers in defining which literacy standards were most important for ensuring student success.

In addition to issues of curricular viability, Marzano (2003) noted many typical public schools did not offer a "guaranteed" curriculum. Often, students (and their parents) navigate a patchwork of rigor because the academic expectations in one classroom are not equivalent to the expectations in the classroom next door. Similarly, the mathematics concepts taught to fourth-grade students (even if learned well) are not challenging enough to guarantee students will be prepared for the fifth-grade math classes down the hall. Likewise, the concepts and skills learned by students in English II are not guaranteed to build upon (without repetition) the concepts learned by students in English I. Often, the lack of a guaranteed curriculum compels parents to lobby principals, urging them to assign their children to teachers who have a reputation for teaching rigorous academic content that will enable their children to succeed in subsequent grade levels.

In contrast, in NCUST's award-winning schools, leadership teams have helped teachers establish a clear, logical roadmap, designed to lead all students to master a defined set of important, rigorous academic concepts and skills. America's Best Schools offer students (and their parents) a guaranteed curriculum that ensures every student (regardless of classroom assignment) has the opportunity to learn essential academic content (Johnson, Uline, & Perez, 2017, 2019; Johnson, Uline, & Munro, 2023). Students in any sixth-grade math class at Stillman Middle School (Vignette H) will learn the same key concepts and skills students learn in other sixth-grade math classes at the school. Furthermore, students in all the sixth-grade math classes will have a high likelihood of being prepared to succeed the following year in seventh-grade math with whichever teachers are assigned to teach the course. Similarly, literacy instruction for third-grade students at Wynnebrook Elementary (Vignette G) is designed to ensure students will have a high likelihood of success in whichever fourth-grade class they are assigned.

To create rigorous, viable, and guaranteed curricula, leadership teams endeavor to accomplish the following. First, leadership teams strive to generate shared understandings among educators about the essential concepts and skills all students should learn at each grade level or in each course. Second, leadership teams ensure their schools maintain rigorous academic expectations for all students, including groups of students who traditionally have not experienced academic success. Finally, leadership teams ensure that learning expectations build logically and reasonably from one grade level to the next, so students enjoy a high likelihood of academic success as they transition from one level to the next.

## *Leadership Teams Generated Consensus About the Essential Concepts and Skills All Students Should Learn*

In NCUST's award-winning schools, leaders recognized that efforts to cover objectives or standards were only useful to the degree they led students to understand and master essential concepts and skills. Generally, leadership teams rejected the notion that teachers should "cover" all state standards, professional standards, or objectives addressed in a textbook if there was insufficient time to teach the content in ways that led students to deep understanding and mastery. Instead, leadership teams engaged educators in working together to determine which concepts and skills students needed to master in order to have a high likelihood of success at the next grade level or in the next course in the sequence.

Administrators and teachers worked together to ensure teachers who taught the same grade level or the same course shared a commitment to teaching their students the same concepts and skills. Moreover, leadership teams often made sure teachers shared similar understandings of what students should be able to accomplish to demonstrate deep understanding or mastery of the standard. For example, at Wynnebrook Elementary (Vignette G), third-grade students could solve multiplication problems, and they could explain why multiplication made sense. At Stillman Middle School (Vignette H), students could describe the concepts they were learning in biology and explain how the concepts were important to the survival of cells and organisms.

As Principal Berry from Wynnebrook Elementary explained:

> So, we would have these discussions and say, "Okay, here is your standard, but what does that actually mean?" And it was so eye-opening to see one standard, one sentence, and see how many ways teachers at the same grade level viewed what the standard meant. So, we'd look at a standard and say, "Okay, what does this verb mean in this standard?" We talked about how we had to make sure the kids knew how to do whatever was required. And to this day, I think that's what continues to make us successful.
>
> (Johnson et al., 2023, p. 44)

Teachers are less likely to feel efficacious if they believe they don't have time to help their students master the essential concepts and skills that are building blocks for further learning within a discipline. Teachers are more likely to feel efficacious if they believe they are being asked to help their students master a reasonable number of challenging concepts and skills. By establishing curricula that teachers perceived as viable, leadership teams advanced teacher collective efficacy.

## Leadership Teams Insisted Upon High Levels of Academic Rigor for All Students

Although leaders in NCUST's award-winning schools did not necessarily endeavor to teach their students all standards or objectives, it is important to note that leaders committed to ensuring their students would master content perceived as academically rigorous and intellectually challenging. Department chairs, grade-level leaders, school administrators, and other leadership team members insisted their students could and should learn rigorous concepts and skills that were essential to success at the next grade level, in the next course, or at the next school or post-secondary level. A principal of one NCUST award-winning school explained:

> Our demographics do not give us permission to offer our students less than students get in wealthier communities. In fact, our demographics demand that we teach more so that we give our students realistic opportunities to compete in life. Our students will learn more only if we structure our classes so that students learn content that is just as rigorous as the content learned in schools in wealthy communities. Why not give our students the same challenges, the same opportunities? If we don't, who will?
>
> (Johnson et al., 2017, p. 37)

Creating a viable curriculum did not mean creating a weak or easy curriculum. In fact, many teachers at NCUST award-winning schools explained state standards were a starting point as they deliberated about the content their students should learn. Often, the deliberations led teachers to commit to teaching even more rigorous concepts and skills.

As a result, in hundreds of classrooms in NCUST award-winning schools, we found lessons designed to lead students to demonstrate they could analyze relationships, identify examples and counterexamples, ascertain patterns, distinguish differences, generate reasonable predictions, justify those predictions with evidence, apply concepts to solve real problems, and evaluate their answers.

Teachers sought to ensure their students could demonstrate the higher-order thinking skills associated with the standards/objectives they identified as sufficiently rigorous. So, when a student correctly solved for x, the teacher might ask, "Why does that answer make sense?" or "Can you think of a real situation when you might need to solve for x in this manner?" When a student correctly remembered the year of an important event, the teacher might have responded, "Excellent! What else was happening during the time period that might have influenced why the event occurred that year?" Or, when a student correctly predicted which character in the story demonstrated courage and integrity, the teacher might have responded, "Great prediction! What actions did the character take earlier in the story that might have led you to predict she would demonstrate such courage and integrity?"

Standards and objectives were not merely written on charts or whiteboards as an appeasement to visiting administrators. Instead, teachers breathed life into their learning expectations by leading all their students to engage, think, and make sense of concepts. Teachers seemed determined to ensure all their students would experience progress in advancing toward the standard or objective each day.

In NCUST award-winning schools, educators "shared a clear vision for the success of all their students" (Theokas, González, Manriquez, & Johnson, 2019, p. 68). Frequently, students (including students emerging as multi-lingual, students with histories of behavior issues, students who started the year below grade level, students with Individual Education Plans, and many other students) observed specific ways they were included in their teacher's vision of genuine academic success. Elementary students heard their daily academic conversations as evidence of their ability to discuss academic concepts intelligently. Middle school students recognized the reports they were developing as similar to the work performed by their high school siblings. High school students saw how the concepts they were learning prepared them to succeed in dual-enrollment courses, advanced placement courses, or career-technology programs that provided industry certifications. As a result, the school's learning culture transformed how students perceived themselves and their chances of academic success. Rigorous curricula contributed to this positive transformational culture.

## *Leadership Teams Generated Clarity About the Vertical Path to Success in Each Discipline*

When students perform well at one level yet can be reliably predicted to perform poorly at the next, this result suggests the curricula are not adequately guaranteed. A passing grade in English I should indicate a student has acquired the concepts and has demonstrated the skills necessary to have a high likelihood of success in English II. A guaranteed curriculum should ensure that when students learn the essential concepts and skills expected for one level, they are on the path to succeed at subsequent levels, from preschool through dual-enrollment or advanced placement courses.

At NCUST award-winning schools, leadership teams engaged teacher teams in working vertically (across grade levels or across course levels) to ensure student success was facilitated by excellent planning, as students matriculated from one grade to the next or from one course to the subsequent course in a sequence. For example, in a school where most 10th-grade students took biology and most 11th-grade students took chemistry, the chemistry teachers might ask the teachers who teach 10th-grade mathematics (or those who teach biology to 10th-grade students) if they could ensure their students learned how to make unit conversations (especially metric conversations) using scientific notation.

By planning across grade levels, teachers worked together to maximize the likelihood students would succeed with increasingly challenging academic content. As a student at Young Men's Leadership Academy (Vignette B) explained, "At some schools, it is like they [the teachers] set you up to fail, but here, at YMLA, it's like they've tried to set us up to succeed."

## Why Establishing Rigorous Curricula Is Challenging Yet Rewarding

Changing what is taught in schools is difficult because often systems do not ensure teachers understand clearly what their students need to learn. Many teacher preparation programs do not teach prospective educators what state standards mean or what sorts of student work demonstrate the attainment of those standards. Often, when teachers are hired, administrators assume new teachers understand the standards and how to teach them. Rarely do teachers have opportunities to talk with each other about what standards imply and what students should be able to demonstrate when they have met standards. In some districts, teachers are told if they follow the district-adopted textbook, they will teach the standards (de facto) because the textbook is aligned to the standards. And yet, if the teacher doesn't know the destination at which her students are expected to arrive, it is much more difficult for her to ascertain if the textbook is an adequate or appropriate tool for ensuring the students' success.

Changing what is taught is also difficult because of the way schools structure the use of time. Most schools depend upon multiple professionals and paraprofessionals (i.e., teachers at various grade levels, specialists in English language development, school counselors, reading specialists, instructional aides, specialists in supporting students with disabilities) to work together to bring each of their students to a deep understanding of a set of complex, challenging concepts and skills. Logically, schools would structure time for these educators to plan collaboratively how they might use their collective knowledge of the students, the content, and the learning outcomes to ensure student success. However, in many schools, collaboration is minimal, episodic, or dependent on the willingness of individuals to work extra, unpaid hours. In many schools, when time is set aside for collaboration, the time is not used to deepen everyone's understanding of what students need to learn and what might be the best ways to ensure excellent learning for all students.

The way schools structure the school day for students often presents another barrier to ensuring rigorous curricula for all. Oakes (1985) demonstrated that ability-level tracks did not serve students well and often became ruts that trapped Black/African American and Latino/Hispanic students in curricula that failed to provide them opportunities to develop their thinking skills and academic abilities. However, 40 years later, many schools continue to schedule students by ability groups, from which they rarely escape. In many schools, large percentages of students are denied opportunities to learn more challenging academic content and skills because structures (e.g., master schedules) are based on invalid assumptions about the need for ability grouping.

Teacher beliefs about the abilities of students to learn challenging content presents another key factor inhibiting curricular change in schools. Irvine and Fraser (1998), Bondy and Ross (2008), and Ladson-Billings (2002) found that teachers who insisted their students perform to high standards (teachers who were "warm demanders") were more likely to generate high levels of academic success, especially among students of color. Nonetheless, many teachers and administrators today believe they are being kind and supportive when they shield students from rigorous curricula and allow them "to succeed" with curricula that do not provide opportunities to learn grade-level concepts and skills. In many schools, educators do not provide students opportunities to learn more rigorous curricula because educators convince themselves they are serving students better by teaching concepts and skills that are substantially easier than the concepts students will need to understand to succeed in the next grade level or the next course.

Often, the greatest reason schools fail to provide all students challenging, rigorous curricula is that administrators are convinced their students will learn more if they ensure teachers thoroughly address every standard prescribed by their state. Although this belief is well intentioned, the belief has never been supported with substantial evidence. In many states, only half of all students (and far fewer students of color) demonstrate proficiency on state assessments of standards, even though many schools push teachers to address all state standards. National Assessment of Educational Progress results indicate that only one-third of students demonstrate proficiency in reading and mathematics. In every one of the 174 schools that have earned NCUST's awards, educators teach their students more rigorous concepts and skills than those taught at similar schools and to students who come from similar families. Often without covering all state standards, without adhering to district scope and sequence calendars, and without following with fidelity the scripted programs used in other schools, educators in NCUST award-winning schools lead their students to outperform statewide averages on many measures, including state assessments.

In too many schools, "covering content" has become a euphemism for teaching. When "I covered it" is equivalent to saying, "I taught it," we reduce the art and science of teaching to the mechanics of moving through a series of scripted lessons, textbook pages, or paper and/or electronic worksheets. Many schools fail to provide students rich, rigorous curricula because systems focus more on covering everything than on helping teachers teach important things well.

Learning rigorous academic content is essential for every student who hopes to earn a living wage in today's economy, who wants to become an informed consumer, who wants to communicate and collaborate with others in ways that both demonstrate respect and generate respect, and who wants to participate wisely and efficaciously in democratic processes. Nonetheless, many schools today do not offer significant numbers of their students the opportunity to learn essential rigorous concepts and skills. Table 4.1 summarizes the challenges associated with establishing rigorous curricula but also specifies the rewards gained when leadership teams address those challenges well.

Table 4.1 Challenges and Rewards of Establishing Rigorous Curricula

| Issue | The Challenges | The Rewards |
|---|---|---|
| **Generating consensus about the essential concepts and skills all students should learn.** | Often teachers have different notions about what students should learn related to a discipline at specific grade levels or in specific courses. Generating consensus is essential, but it requires a substantial investment in both time and leadership. Teachers need time to work together (typically in professional learning committees) to create shared understandings about what students need to learn. | When schools set aside time for teams to work together to ensure educators share common understandings about what students need to learn, everyone can aim toward the same learning target, and educators can support each other in achieving the target. |
| **Generating consensus about the essential concepts and skills all students should learn.** | Often teachers feel pressured to cover all state standards, all learning objectives, all the chapters of the textbook. When those pressures prevail, often the curriculum is not viable. Teachers may rush to "get through" content rather than ensuring their students learn essential content. | When the pressure to cover everything is removed, teachers can focus on what is essential for students to learn. Then it becomes easier for teachers to plan to ensure their students learn what's essential. |
| **Generating consensus about the essential concepts and skills all students should learn.** | In some schools, there is little discussion about standards because the focus is on following a textbook, a scope and sequence, a scripted program, or a piece of software. In such cases, teachers feel compelled to "follow the program" rather than ensuring their students learn essential concepts and skills. | When the focus shifts from "following the program" to teaching essential concepts and skills, teachers are more likely to use programs, textbooks, and so on as tools to help their students learn what they need to learn. |

*(Continued)*

Table 4.1 (Continued)

| Issue | The Challenges | The Rewards |
|---|---|---|
| **Insisting upon high levels of academic rigor for all students.** | When classes are structured based on ability groupings, teachers may assume it is inappropriate to teach challenging content to students who are placed in lower groups. | When ability groupings are minimized or eliminated, everyone is more likely to share responsibility for teaching challenging content to all students. |
| **Insisting upon high levels of academic rigor for all students.** | Teachers may believe their students are incapable of learning rigorous content, so they might feel as if they are being insensitive or cruel if they push their students to learn challenging content. Teachers may need help to see how students can be taught to achieve high levels of academic rigor. | Collective teacher efficacy is born when teachers begin to recognize their ability to help all student groups grasp challenging academic concepts. |
| **Generating clarity about the vertical path to success in each discipline.** | Teachers may have little knowledge about the learning expectations at the grades below or above the grade they teach. In most schools, there is no deliberate effort to structure communication among vertical teams of teachers. | Collective teacher efficacy is enhanced and accelerated when teachers understand how their efforts contribute to student success in subsequent grades. Teachers are more likely to see themselves as part of a team that leads students to important academic successes. |

# Rigorous Curricula: What It Is and What It Isn't

(X) **What It Isn't: An Afternoon Professional Development Session Led by Administrators About Standards and Curricular Expectations**

> Traditional professional development sessions about standards and learning expectations are inadequate unless they lead to ongoing, regular discussions among teachers about the learning expectations their students need to achieve and what those expectations mean students should know and be able to do.

(✓) **What It Is: Developing Regular, Ongoing Opportunities for Educators to Work Together to Develop Common Understandings of What Specific Standards Mean and What Students Should Be Able to Accomplish When They Achieve Mastery of the Standards**

> Regular, ongoing collaboration focused on developing common understandings of standards should be a part of teacher's weekly schedule. Educators who teach the same grade level or the same course should meet frequently to ensure they share an understanding of what each standard implies their students need to learn. Additionally, special education personnel, reading specialists, mathematics specialists, paraprofessionals, and other support personnel should have opportunities to be part of collaborative conversations about essential learning expectations.

(X) **What It Isn't: Insisting Educators Follow a Textbook, Scripted Program, or Technology-Based Program, Without Ensuring Teachers Understand Specifically How the Program Is Intended to Help Students Master Essential Standards, Objectives, or Learning Expectations**

> When leaders ask teachers to follow the textbook, scripted program, or software without question, leaders may be inadvertently asking teachers to stop thinking about what their students need to learn and how to help their students learn. Leaders may be asking the professionals they have hired to relinquish responsibility for advancing learning and to assume responsibility for

blindly following the lead of program authors who never met the students being served.

### ✓ What It Is: Supporting Educators in Wisely Using Existing Textbooks, Workbooks, Scope and Sequence Charts, and Other Curricular Tools and in Creating/Adapting and Using New Curricular Tools to Help Their Students Master Essential Concepts and Skills

In NCUST award-winning schools, leadership teams are less likely to seek the perfect curricular tools, because (1) they realize no tool is perfect for all students and (2) they believe intelligent, caring, and empowered teachers will use tools wisely to help students master challenging concepts. Leadership teams in award-winning schools support teachers in determining how they can best use the strengths of certain curricular tools and how they can best use, adapt, or create other tools that can advance their students' mastery of essential concepts and skills.

### ✗ What It Isn't: Structuring Classes So Some Students Are Taught The Concepts and Skills Essential for Building Future Academic Successes, While Students Who Show Less Academic Promise Are Taught Lower-Level Concepts and Skills to Boost Their Self-Esteem

When classes are structured so some students are taught essential grade-level concepts and skills and students perceived to be less capable are taught lower-level concepts and skills, the school diminishes its opportunity to make a positive difference in students' lives. Most students taught in lower-level classes never catch up. Even if they persist to graduation, few learn the concepts, skills, and dispositions necessary to sustain themselves professionally, socially, or economically.

### ✓ What It Is: Structuring Classes So All Students Have Excellent Learning Opportunities and Effective Support That Helps Them Master the Concepts and Skills Essential for Building Future Academic Successes

In NCUST award-winning schools, some teachers have said, "I'm not sure how I will get this group of students to achieve our school's high expectations, but I know there has to be a way. And as a team, we won't give up!" This positive attitude is reflected in how students are grouped for learning (from pre-kindergarten through advanced placement courses). Through carefully designed differentiated approaches, teachers aim to help all their students achieve mastery of essential concepts and skills. As teachers challenge all their students to master rigorous academic concepts and skills, they provide abundant, high-quality support to ensure students succeed.

## (X) What It Isn't: Ignoring Evidence That Suggests Some Educators Do Not Believe Groups of Students They Serve Are Capable of Mastering Challenging Academic Concepts and Skills

When educators observe the academic frustration experienced by some of their students, educators may understandably question whether some students can meet challenging academic expectations. Some may sincerely believe some groups of students should not be expected to achieve grade-level standards. Often leadership teams ignore this lack of belief and reinforce it by watering down learning expectations for certain groups of students. When leaders ignore the lack of belief in students' capacity to succeed academically, they diminish the likelihood the school will ever generate positive learning outcomes for all students. Equally counterproductive, some leadership teams shame and blame educators who articulate a lack of belief in their students' ability to learn challenging concepts and skills. Such leadership responses only cause teachers to be more cautious or more rebellious.

## (✓) What It Is: Continuously Supporting Educators in Nurturing the Belief That All Groups of Students Can and Will Master Challenging Academic Concepts and Skills When They Provide Effective, Engaging Instruction

Many leaders of NCUST award-winning schools reported they had or have educators who questioned whether their students could achieve the rigorous academic expectations articulated by the school's leadership team. Typically, in the award-winning schools, disbelief was not ignored, nor was it addressed in an aggressive, confrontational manner. Instead, leadership teams worked first to help ensure educators had abundant opportunities to see students (from all groups) successfully mastering challenging academic concepts and skills. Leadership teams helped educators feel like they had excellent support committed to helping them refine their practices in ways that would lead all their students to master rigorous curricular expectations. Leadership teams in NCUST award-winning schools changed educators' beliefs by supporting educators in improving learning results for all their students.

### (X) What It Isn't: Nurturing a Culture in Which Educators Blame Students, Parents, or Their Colleague Educators When Students Were Not Prepared Well to Master Challenging Academic Concepts and Skills

In some schools, when students enter a grade level or a course, there is often negative discourse about the students' lack of preparation for the academic content the students will need to master. Often the discourse blames last year's teachers, students, or the students' parents. Such negative discourse diminishes collective teacher efficacy and fosters suspicion and division.

### (✓) What It Is: Nurturing a Culture in Which Educators Work Together to Create Seamless Transitions Between Grade Levels or Courses That Maximize the Likelihood All Students Will Be Well Prepared to Master the Challenging Academic Concepts and Skills Taught at the Next Grade Level or in the Next Course

In NCUST award-winning schools, most students enter the next grade or course well prepared to succeed academically. Success, however, is planned. Leadership teams ensure teachers coordinate vertically throughout their schools (across grade levels or across courses within a discipline) to ensure teachers understand specifically what students will need to master in order to have a high likelihood of academic success at the next level. Teams of teachers use information from this vertical articulation to ensure their students master the requisite concepts and skills. Often, teams were proud of their successes in ensuring their students were "more than ready" for the next level.

## Tips for Leadership Teams

### *How Schools Can Advance Rigorous Curricula (Remember to Review and Implement These Tips Regularly)*

- Ensure educators who teach students in the same grade level (or students in the same courses) have frequent, regular opportunities to work together to build common understandings of the essential concepts and skills their students need to learn. While these meetings should certainly include classroom teachers, it is also helpful when other teachers (e.g., special education personnel, reading specialists, English language development personnel, math specialists, paraprofessionals, and others) participate in ways that allow them to share in developing these common understandings.

- Engage educators in discussions to ensure they know they are not required to cover more content than they can reasonably help their students master during the semester/school year. Develop a school-wide shared understanding of the essential concepts and skills students need to master at each grade level or in each course. Help teachers understand why ensuring students master the essential concepts and skills is far more useful than covering all standards, all learning objectives, or all chapters of the textbook.

- Engage educators in discussions with their colleagues across grade levels to ensure the essential concepts and skills associated with each grade level or course will prepare students to succeed in subsequent grade levels or courses. Nurture the expectation that success in one grade level will become much more likely when students meet the essential expectations articulated for students in the prior grade.

- Regularly engage teachers in revisiting their lists of essential concepts and skills associated with each grade level or course. Refine the lists to ensure greater horizontal alignment (teachers who teach the same grade or course share similar understandings of learning expectations) and vertical alignment (teachers share similar understandings of how the learning expectations at one grade support student success in meeting the learning expectations at the next grade).

- Prioritize the development and implementation of job-embedded professional development to help teachers understand how they can use curricular tools wisely to increase students' mastery of essential concepts and skills. Reduce or eliminate the expectation that teachers use curricular tools religiously and elevate the expectation that teachers use curricular tools wisely to help their students master essential concepts and skills. Empower teachers to make smart decisions about when and how to veer away from textbooks, workbooks, or other common tools.

- As a leadership team, continuously strive to help educators see evidence of students achieving mastery of challenging concepts and skills. Especially, highlight evidence of mastery among student groups that have been underserved. Nurture a school-wide belief that all student groups can master challenging academic concepts and skills.

## Where Is Your School on the Road to Developing Rigorous Curricula?

The school leadership team should consider using the rubric in Table 4.2 to assess the school's progress toward developing rigorous curricula. By reviewing the rubric each semester, the leadership team may identify and celebrate areas of growth and identify areas where additional growth is needed.

Rigorous Curricula

Table 4.2 Rubric for Assessing Progress Developing Rigorous Curricula

| | Blazing New Paths of Equity/Excellence (Exemplary) | Entering a Whole New Environment (Approaching) | At Early Mile Markers (Developing) | At the Highway On-Ramp (Waiting) |
|---|---|---|---|---|
| Generating consensus about the essential concepts and skills all students should learn. | Educators are not merely committed to "covering" the essential concepts and skills. They are committed to ensuring their students achieve mastery. Even when there is substantial evidence of success, educators refine and raise expectations. | Educators who teach the same grade or course similarly define mastery of the concepts and skills their students should learn. With a shared vision of the learning targets they want students to achieve, educators support each other in elevating rigor. | Educators who teach the same grade or course agree upon the essential concepts and skills all their students should learn. | Educators who teach the same grade or course pursue different learning expectations. |
| Insisting upon high levels of academic rigor for all students. | Even when there is substantial evidence that all student groups are mastering grade-level concepts and skills, educators engage in deliberate efforts to learn how they can successfully raise curricular expectations. | Ongoing efforts are made to help educators see that all groups of students can master essential concepts and skills for their grade level when the students receive effective, engaging instruction. | All students are taught in classes or groups where they will have real opportunities to learn essential concepts and skills for their grade level. | Some groups of students are in classes or groups where they are not likely to be taught essential concepts and skills for their grade level. Some educators do not believe their students are capable of learning grade-level concepts and skills. |

(Continued)

Table 4.2 (Continued)

| | Blazing New Paths of Equity/Excellence (Exemplary) | Entering a Whole New Environment (Approaching) | At Early Mile Markers (Developing) | At the Highway On-Ramp (Waiting) |
|---|---|---|---|---|
| **Generating clarity about the vertical path to success in each discipline.** | Even when there is evidence that all student groups are mastering the concepts and skills specified for each grade level/course, educators continuously seek to refine and elevate expectations in ways that enhance students' academic success. | Educators throughout the school believe the agreed-upon learning expectations are logical and reasonable. Educators perceive their chances of success will be enhanced by the efforts of their colleagues at other grade levels. | Educators have contributed to and agreed upon a set of learning expectations that articulate the concepts and skills students should master at each grade level or in each course. | Learning expectations for grade levels or courses are not explicit. Often, teachers think they are preparing students to succeed at the next level, but they are not. |

# References

Bondy, E., & Ross, D. D. (2008). The teacher as warm demander. *Educational Leadership, 66*(1), 54–58.

Education Trust. (2020). *Social, emotional, and academic development through an equity lens*. Washington, DC: Education Trust.

Irvine, J. J., & Fraser, J. W. (1998). Warm demanders. *Education Week, 17*(35), 56.

Johnson, J. F., Uline, C. L., & Munro, S. J. (2023). *When Black students excel: How schools can engage and empower Black students*. New York: Routledge and Taylor & Francis Group.

Johnson, J. F., Uline, C. L., & Perez, L. (2017). *Leadership in America's best urban schools*. New York: Routledge and Taylor & Francis Group.

Johnson, J. F., Uline, C. L., & Perez, L. (2019). *Teaching practices from America's best urban schools: A guide for school and classroom leaders*. New York: Routledge and Taylor & Francis Group.

Ladson-Billings, G. (2002). I ain't writin' nuttin': Permissions to fail and demands to succeed in urban classrooms. In L. Delpit & J. K. Dowdy (Eds.), *The skin that we speak: Thoughts on language and culture in the classroom* (pp. 107–120). New York: The New Press.

Marzano, R. J. (2003). *What works in schools: Translating research into action*. Alexandria, VA: ASCD.

Oakes, J. (1985). *Keeping track: How schools structure inequalities*. New Haven, CT: Yale University Press.

Pane, J. F., Griffin, B. A., McCaffrey, D. F., & Karam, R. (2015). *Effectiveness of cognitive tutor algebra I at scale*. American Institutes for Research.

Theokas, C., González, M. L., Manriquez, C., & Johnson, J. F. (2019). *Five practices for improving the success of Latino students: A guide for secondary school leaders*. New York: Routledge and Taylor & Francis Group.

# 5 | Effective Initial Instruction

**Voices of Students and Parents From America's Best Schools**

"I attended PS 171 (Patrick Henry Prep) from 2016–2019, 6–8th grade. I'm from a family of five, supported by one income. The music program at PS 171 cultivated my love and hunger for the arts and I wanted to be fully immersed. Mr. D helped me participate in competitions. I wanted to sing classical professionally. I am also a big STEM girl. At 171, teachers such as Ms. R and Mr. J not only supported me in math and science but also helped me believe I was just as capable as anyone. Ms. R became a second mother to me, nurturing my love of science and my dreams of being in the medicine field. Her Living Environments class expanded my love of science and made me confident in what I wanted to do. Currently, I'm at the University of Michigan double majoring in vocal performance and biochemistry."

– Amaya, former P.S. 171 student

"My teachers at Silver Wing had an impact on me. I can't say I'm a straight A student. It wasn't easy for me. The teachers would help me a lot. They knew I needed to get out of my comfort zone and talk more. They helped me talk a lot about what I was learning. They helped me a lot with homework. They helped me become prepared for middle school and high school. Because of my teachers and my principal at Silver Wing, I'm graduating from high school now and I will go to Southwestern College."

– Ricardo, former student at Silver Wing Elementary

"Born in the Philippines, I was just seven years old when I moved to East Harlem and had to learn to live in a diverse community and navigate the rigorous curriculum at Patrick Henry. I am grateful [to the teachers for] providing an abundance of opportunities for me [to grow and succeed], while establishing a safe and welcoming environment. For example, I participated in the 'Day with a Scientist Program' at Mt. Sinai Hospital in NYC. We participated in dissections and lessons related to the medical field under the guidance of medical personnel. Because of my successes at Patrick Henry and the goals I have achieved, I now attend the Bronx High School of Science, one of the city's nine specialized high schools."

– Cory, former P.S. 171 student

# VIGNETTE I: P.S. 171, Patrick Henry Preparatory School, New York City Department of Education, East Harlem, New York

### WON NCUST'S AMERICA'S BEST SCHOOL AWARD IN 2018 AND 2023

*Over 80% of the students at P.S. 171 (Patrick Henry Preparatory School) identify as Black/African American or Latino/Hispanic, and over 70% meet free- or reduced-price lunch criteria. Over 80% demonstrate proficiency on New York State's assessments in English language arts, and over 90% demonstrate proficiency on the state's mathematics assessments (far exceeding statewide averages). The heart of the success of this public East Harlem school is effective initial teaching (referred to as "core teaching" at Patrick Henry) that has been continuously refined through the work of both administrative and teacher leaders.*

Patrick Henry teachers believe their students can achieve and exceed New York's academic standards, as long as they work together to deliver clear, engaging, and relevant instruction. Their confidence is fortified by the belief that their colleagues are eager to support them as they work to find ways to excite their students about learning challenging concepts and skills. As well, their conviction is reinforced by their perception that the school's administrators trust them to make wise, data-informed decisions about their instruction practices. Principal Aharon Schultz emphasized that teachers at Patrick Henry have chosen to spend considerably more time working together to improve instructional organization and delivery than teachers at most other schools.

A major topic of collaboration (from elementary grades through middle school grades) has been the selection of the novels grade-level teams use to teach English language arts standards, as well as important social studies standards. For example, the sixth-grade team chose Tristan Strong Punches a Hole in the Sky by Kwame Mbalia, a novel that combines African American folklore and West African mythology in a manner that related to current, real-world issues. The seventh-grade team chose Barren Grounds by David Robertson because it provided abundant opportunities to engage students in discussions about important English language arts concepts and skills while simultaneously addressing important social studies standards. The eighth-grade team chose We Are Not From Here by Jenny Torres Sanchez and The Hate U Give by Angela Thomas. Teachers recognized that their students were much more likely to understand and master challenging academic standards if they utilized literature students found interesting and relevant to their lives.

Teachers planned how they would use the novels to engage students in thoughtful dialogue that prompted the thinking required by state standards. Teachers chose books their students would be eager to read, discuss, and dissect. Students were more likely to demonstrate their ability to model strong literacy skills when they saw the content as relevant to their lives. Beyond academic concerns, the novels emphasized empathy, understanding, and civic responsibility in ways that nurtured Patrick Henry's positive school culture.

At Patrick Henry, teachers also use collaboration time to monitor students' progress toward mastery. Teachers work together to plan assessments or performances that require students to demonstrate their levels of understanding. For example, the eighth-grade team required students to write a culminating essay on New York City's Right-to-Shelter laws. Students had to draw from various works (including We Are Not From Here) to substantiate their claims. Additionally, students engaged in a debate in which they had opportunities to justify their written arguments in a productive discourse.

Many Patrick Henry teachers claimed their classroom assessments and projects have become more rigorous over the years. Simultaneously, student work products and state assessment data reveal that Patrick Henry students are more successful than ever. When asked why their higher expectations did not result in lower rates of student success, one teacher responded, "Yes, we embrace high expectations because we want our students to be able to compete in the world, but then we plan a quality of instruction that will ensure our students will succeed." Another teacher concurred, saying, "We expect ourselves to work as a team to create clear, relevant, powerful learning experiences that lead all our students to success."

## VIGNETTE J: Silver Wing Elementary School, Chula Vista, California

### WON NCUST'S AMERICA'S BEST SCHOOL AWARD IN 2020

*Only four miles north of the U.S./Mexico border crossing, students at Silver Wing Elementary outperform students in most California elementary schools. Educators at Silver Wing do not perceive family income (over 80% of Silver Wing students meet low-income criteria) or language background (approximately 60% of the students are emerging as multi-lingual learners) as reasons to lower expectations. Instead, educators throughout Silver Wing expect their students to demonstrate mastery of very challenging academic concepts and skills.*

*Principal Corona credits Silver Wing teachers and the school's Instructional Leadership Team (ILT) for the school's academic successes. With a representative from each grade level (from kindergarten through grade 6), the ILT assumes responsibility for building a schoolwide instructional approach that will prepare all Silver Wing students to be academically successful in middle school and beyond. Principal Corona explained, "The ILT is committed to helping all our teachers help our students succeed." Conversely, the ILT credits Principal Corona for the school's success. One ILT leader explained, "She [Principal Corona] trusts us as professionals who are going to do whatever needs to happen to make sure our students get what they need." The mutual respect, combined with a deep commitment to improving the lives of students, is a cornerstone of the school's success.*

*The mutual respect creates a climate in which educators feel supported as they work to shape instruction that helps students at each grade level advance toward mastery of challenging concepts and skills through listening, speaking, reading, and writing. Principal Corona and the ILT have helped Silver Wing educators understand how they can create positive learning environments in which their students will have abundant, rich opportunities to derive meaning from a variety of types of texts, engage in thoughtful conversations about important concepts and skills, and demonstrate their thinking through effective writing. Silver Wing teachers (at every grade level) have been supported in adapting traditional "stand-and-deliver" instructional approaches. Instead, teachers have learned how to promote student collaborative conversations so all their students are more likely to engage thoughtfully in every lesson and demonstrate their thinking in ways that become increasingly sophisticated as students advance toward sixth grade.*

*At Silver Wing, mutual respect has also influenced a gradual approach to instructional change. Both the principal and the ILT limit the focus of improvement efforts to only a small number of instructional issues. Teachers believe the focus gives them realistic opportunities to try new approaches, receive constructive feedback from their peers, and begin to develop expertise. Most importantly, teachers see the benefits of their improvement efforts in the learning outcomes of their students. ILT leaders indicated teacher turnover at Silver Wing is much lower than many schools that serve similar student populations, in part because, "Together, we know we are making a difference for our students. We help each other succeed, so that our students will succeed. We wouldn't want to work anywhere else."*

---

First, the bad news. If all the previously mentioned gears (effective leadership teams, positive transformational culture, and rigorous curricula) move smoothly and substantially, yet instruction remains the same, student learning outcomes are not likely to improve. In the absence of improved instruction, student groups that previously performed at low levels are likely to continue to perform at low levels. The energy from all the other gears must work to ensure all students benefit from effective instruction.

Effective instruction is instruction that results in students mastering the rigorous concepts and skills they need to learn to pursue their academic, civic, and career goals successfully. If instruction does not lead a group of students to master critical, rigorous concepts and skills, instruction for those students is ineffective. At Patrick Henry Preparatory School (Vignette K), teachers knew they had to shape instruction around literature that their East Harlem students would find engaging and relevant. At Silver Wing Elementary (Vignette L), teachers knew they needed to design instruction to maximize the likelihood that students who did not speak English at home would have outstanding opportunities to practice listening, speaking, reading, and writing in ways that deepened their understanding of challenging academic standards. Effective instruction ensures that all groups of students have a strong likelihood of mastering important academic concepts and skills.

Now, the good news. If all the previously mentioned gears (effective leadership teams, positive transformational culture, and rigorous curricula) move smoothly and substantially, improvements in instruction are much more likely to have powerful impact. Each of the previously mentioned gears will transfer energy and power in ways that will help schools become learning organizations (Senge et al., 2012) that continuously improve the power of instruction and lead students to master challenging concepts and skills. Furthermore, the movement of the other gears will build the capacity of the school to improve the effectiveness of initial instruction: the instruction provided to students when teachers first endeavor to lead students to master a specific concept or skill.

Of course, teachers in all schools provide initial instruction. However, in many schools, there is little effort to ensure that initial instruction is effective for all students and all student groups. Low success rates from one semester or one academic year rarely lead to an improvement of the core teaching practices educators use every day to help students learn important concepts and skills. Instead, low success rates may lead to a cacophony of blaming, a new textbook adoption, additional testing, or more intervention (e.g., a revision of the master schedule so that some students spend greater amounts of time experiencing frustration with the subjects they hate the most). In NCUST award-winning schools, however, leadership teams pursue comprehensive, sustained efforts to support teachers in providing initial instruction that is likely to lead all students to deeper understanding of important concepts and skills.

## What Leadership Teams Accomplished to Promote Effective Initial Instruction

Many well-intentioned leaders (superintendents, principals, and teacher leaders) have struggled and failed to improve the effectiveness of initial instruction because they did not adequately address the aforementioned gears that could have facilitated their success. Improving the effectiveness of instruction requires the development of trust (as emphasized in the effective leadership team gear). As well, instruction is not likely to improve (beyond token compliance) unless school personnel feel they are working in a positive transformational culture where their colleagues and administrators value them, respect their professionalism, and are sincerely committed to helping them succeed. Additionally, the improvement of instruction is facilitated when teachers have agreed to a focus on a limited set of critical, challenging academic concepts (the curriculum gear). Efforts to improve initial instruction are far less likely to succeed in the absence of an effective leadership team; a positive transformational culture; and guaranteed, viable, and rigorous curricula.

Even when the preceding gears function well, the school-wide improvement of initial instruction is not guaranteed. In NCUST award-winning schools, leadership teams accomplished a few important shifts that accelerated the pace, broadened the reach, and strengthened the power of instructional improvements efforts in ways that influenced more classrooms and more students. To ensure the school-wide improvement of the initial instruction provided to students, leaders focused on instructional issues that had a high likelihood of improving learning outcomes for the groups of students who had previously experienced minimal academic success. As well, the change efforts were limited to a few key instructional practices that would be addressed long term throughout the school. Third, the change efforts were designed to help educators see and appreciate the value of the changes they were being asked to implement. And finally, the changes were designed to help educators believe they had abundant support that would enable them to implement the changes well.

## Leadership Teams Focused on Improvements to Initial Instruction That Mattered for All but Especially Groups Who Had Experienced Minimal Academic Success

In NCUST award-winning schools, the goal is not to improve the use of any or every teaching practice. The goal is to make teaching more effective for the students served, especially for students who frequently have not been served well. Johnson, Uline, and Perez (2019) studied teaching practices in NCUST award-winning schools. Across the many schools that achieved outstanding learning results for all demographic groups, they identified eight prevalent teaching practices. These practices were utilized regularly across subject areas from preschool classes through advanced placement and dual-enrollment courses. The eight practices can be organized into three groups.

First, some practices strengthened the positive transformational culture within classrooms. Specifically, throughout the award-winning schools, educators emphasized practices that led students from all demographic groups to feel valued and capable. Educators supported each other in conceptualizing, implementing, and refining ways of interacting with students that increased the likelihood that all students would feel known, valued, respected, important, intelligent, and loved (Johnson, Uline, & Munro, 2023). As well, educators supported each other in creating learning environments and lesson designs that helped students experience the joy of learning. In many classrooms, disruptive behaviors decreased dramatically and students were more eager to engage in learning activities because they believed their teachers were determined to help them succeed. In his synthesis of meta-analyses related to achievement, Hattie (2023) reported strong effect sizes associated with many of these issues. For example, he noted an effect size of 0.82 with decreasing disruptive behavior, an effect size of 1.03 with teacher credibility (the students' belief that they will learn and succeed with a particular teacher), and an effect size of 0.62 for teacher–student relationships.

The second set of practices strengthened efforts to improve students' access to rigorous curricula. Specifically, teachers planned and delivered instruction in ways that were intended to help all students acquire deep understanding of challenging concepts and skills. Teachers helped their students attain clarity about what they were learning, why it was important, and how they could gauge their learning progress. Continuously, teachers checked each student's understanding of important concepts and skills and used the information acquired to adjust their instructional moves so students were more likely to advance toward mastery. Similarly, Hattie (2023) found strong effect sizes for many of these practices. For example, he reported an effect size of 0.85 for teacher clarity and an effect size of 0.58 for teacher expectations.

The final group of practices maximized the likelihood that all students would be actively engaged in learning. For example, teachers selected instructional materials, specified problems, and identified learning activities that students were likely to perceive as relevant to their interests, backgrounds, and cultures. Students were more likely to see how important academic concepts connected to their experiences, their histories, or their futures. Teachers' voices were heard substantially less than students' voices as teachers taught students to articulate their questions, as well as their answers, through the use of challenging, new vocabulary. Additionally, instead of frustrating students with repetitive, unsuccessful practice, teachers maximized student engagement by skillfully determining (through group discussions, collaborative projects, debates, dramatizations, or other activities) when students were prepared to demonstrate their learning independently. Again, Hattie (2023) found strong effect sizes associated with many of these practices. For example, he reported an effect size of 0.82 for the use of classroom discussion to seek and provide feedback, an effect size of 0.92 for constructivist teaching, and a remarkable effect size of 1.30 for teacher estimates of achievement (the teacher's capacity to ascertain a student's level of understanding and then make appropriate instructional moves).

It is important to note that, in NCUST award-winning schools, leadership teams focused on improvements to initial instruction that would generate better learning outcomes for groups of students who previously had not been well served. It is also important to realize, however, that in every award-winning school, the improvements to initial instruction helped every racial/ethnic group and every income group outperform state averages for all students. Similarly, based upon their studies of meta-analyses of achievement-related variables, Hattie and Zierer (2018, p. xviii) explained, "Certainly, students are marvelously variable and unique, but the simple message was that what worked best tended to work best with most students."

## *Leadership Teams Focused on a Few Key School-Wide Instructional Improvements for Extended Time Periods*

In struggling schools, we have often heard leaders say, "There are so many teaching practices we need to improve in our school. It is hard to know where to start." Seemingly, many leaders try to start everywhere. Each time they provide teachers feedback about instruction, they generate a new "to-do list" with multiple suggestions and/or mandates. In NCUST high-performing school audits, we often ask teachers what their leaders expect to see when they visit classrooms. Often, in struggling schools, teachers either cannot state anything specific about their leaders' expectations or cite long lists of instructional practices they are expected to address. In contrast, in award-winning schools, teachers throughout each school consistently specify two or three important practices that their leaders emphasize. The practices are supported by evidence and connected to the strengths and needs of the students at the school. Professional learning activities are designed to help educators understand and implement the practices. Often, teacher collaboration meetings are structured to emphasize the same two or three practices.

Relatedly, in struggling schools, often teachers express frustration about instructional improvement efforts that change frequently. For example, teachers might explain "Last month, the emphasis was on small-group instruction, and this month, we're working on questioning skills, and the month prior, we learned about the gradual release of responsibility." Often, neither teachers nor administrators could explain the rationale for improvement initiatives that seemed like random acts of professional development. In contrast, in NCUST award-winning schools, teachers, teacher leaders, and administrators described long-term approaches to improving teaching practices. For example, educators at Patrick Henry (Vignette K) described multi-year efforts to help teachers identify compelling novels that enable teachers to teach important academic standards through literature that students found stimulating and relevant to their lives. Similarly, teachers at Silver Wing Elementary (Vignette L) described multiple-year efforts to build teachers' capacity to promote student collaborative conversations.

Multi-year efforts can be important in building the capacity of teachers to implement the practice well enough to be considered a "signature practice" of the school: a practice students can expect to be featured in every classroom. As well, multi-year efforts can be powerful in building the capacity of students to benefit from the practice. For example, at Silver

Wing Elementary, kindergarten teachers work with their students to begin engaging in collaborative academic conversations. Throughout the primary and intermediate grades, teachers help students enhance their ability to articulate their questions, explain their inferences, develop fluency with challenging vocabulary, and justify their conclusions with evidence. When students reach grade 6 at Silver Wing, they are prepared to engage in sophisticated Socratic seminars.

In a sixth-grade Socratic seminar at Silver Wing, involving many emerging multi-lingual learners, a student asked, "On page 18, I see the word 'serum' and I thought a serum was a kind of a liquid that could help you with a sickness or it could endanger you. But that doesn't fit here." Then, another student responded, "Actually, it's on page 19, where it says, 'Books are like truth serum. I think you're right that a serum is usually a liquid, but here, I think the author is trying to say that books act like a serum that helps you see the truth'." The conversation continued for approximately 45 minutes, with every student participating in asking questions and providing answers. Students discussed the novel's use of figurative and literal vocabulary, character motivations, and the author's intent. The teacher listened attentively, took notes about student comments, and engaged only occasionally to focus students on challenging issues. Ultimately, students demonstrated that their Silver Wing experience prepared them to engage in rich academic conversations about literature.

At NCUST award-winning schools, instructional improvement initiatives are not simply strategies for filling the time created by professional development days. Instead, each initiative is an effort to ensure that all students (regardless of classroom assignment) will benefit from a teacher who models the implementation of a powerful instructional strategy in ways that are sufficiently effective to deepen student understanding and elevate learning outcomes.

## Leadership Teams Helped Educators Appreciate the Value of the Desired Instructional Improvements

Even if leadership teams select an outstanding instructional improvement initiative, learning outcomes are not likely to improve if teachers do not understand the instructional improvement and appreciate the reasons the practice can improve teaching and learning when implemented well.

While it is critically important for leadership teams to consider the qualitative and quantitative evidence that might justify a focus upon the teaching practices a school should aim to improve, Hattie and Zierer (2018) emphasized that leaders should not lose sight of why they are endeavoring to improve. Often leaders focus on "what" teachers should improve, with minimal attention to "why" improvement efforts are important. The identification of specific teaching practices to be improved is only a means to pursue the broader goal of improving students' lives.

At each school featured in a vignette in this book, a critical mass of teachers (not necessarily every teacher) could explain the logic behind the major instructional improvement efforts at their school. They could explain why they believed their students would benefit if they invested the time and effort necessary to implement the practice well. Understanding and appreciation of the desired improvements in instructional practices did not occur magically or mysteriously. In NCUST award-winning schools, leadership teams worked with their colleagues to build the desire to improve specific practices (Johnson, Uline, & Perez, 2017). In NCUST award-winning schools (such as the schools featured in the vignettes in this book), leadership teams helped educators understand and appreciate "the why" behind the practices they sought to help teachers implement well.

In contrast, when educators do not understand and appreciate "the why," improvement efforts are far less likely to generate meaningful changes in learning outcomes. Teachers who don't understand why they are changing an instructional practice may be inclined to reduce the practice to a checklist as they try to make sense of "what" they should do to demonstrate their compliance. Leaders who don't understand why they are promoting an instructional practice risk giving credence to compliance checklists and promoting the false goal of "ticking all the checklist boxes" while displacing the real goal of improving student learning.

## Leadership Teams Helped Educators Believe They Had Abundant Time and Support to Learn to Implement Instructional Improvements Well

Even if the leadership team selects an excellent instructional practice, the improvement initiative is not likely to generate improvements in learning outcomes unless teachers believe they have abundant time and support to learn to implement the improvement well (Johnson et al., 2017). In general, our profession grossly underestimates the quantity of time or the quality of support needed to help educators implement important changes well enough to generate improved learning outcomes. In the absence of adequate time and support, some educators are likely to question the motivations of the leaders who promote the practice. Educators may wonder, "Are they really trying to improve learning results, or are they trying to prove I'm not a good teacher? Do they really believe this practice will work for our students, or are they just trying to impress district administrators?"

In NCUST award-winning schools, leadership teams prepared carefully to support their colleagues in learning about and implementing new instructional practices. Leaders helped ensure that educators had abundant opportunities to (1) build a shared understanding of the practice and why it could improve learning outcomes for their students (Fullan, 2011); (2) see and discuss effective implementation and learn how effective implementation differed from less effective or ineffective implementation (Johnson et al., 2017); (3) learn about the conditions that could facilitate or frustrate strong implementation (Johnson et al., 2019); (4) understand how they could monitor their implementation of the practice and the impact on their students (Hattie & Zierer, 2018) so they could make timely adjustments; (5) experience multiple safe opportunities to try the practice with supportive, affirming feedback that acknowledged teachers' progress in implementing the practice (Ross, Lamb, & Johnson, 2023); and (6) receive and reflect upon supportive and affirming feedback in ways that encouraged educators to implement the practice again with even greater impact (Theokas, González, Manriquez, & Johnson, 2019). In the absence of abundant, high-quality, ongoing support that addresses these issues, implementation is less likely to generate better learning outcomes.

## Why Promoting Effective Initial Instruction Is Challenging Yet Rewarding

It may be difficult or impossible to improve learning results for all demographic groups of students without sustained, school-wide improvements in initial instruction. Nonetheless, meaningful improvements are often elusive, in part because leaders at all levels may fail to recognize the complexities of improvement processes.

Bryk, Gomez, Grunow, and LeMahieu (2015) contended that schools, districts, and other educational organizations often rushed to initiate promising new practices yet failed to learn how to promulgate those practices throughout a system. While they described six improvement principles that have important implications, Table 5.1 illustrates how the first three principles help explain why many schools face challenges when they try to improve initial instruction.

First, our profession seems susceptible to solutionitis, "the propensity to jump quickly on a solution before fully understanding the exact problem to be solved" (Bryk et al., 2015, p. 24). Often schools and districts adopt programs, approaches, and other instructional solutions without fully understanding the problem they need to address. If the fundamental problem is that significant numbers of students (or significant numbers of students from specific groups) are not demonstrating understanding of important concepts and skills after initial instruction, a quick change to a new textbook or a new computer-based instructional system may or may not have much potential to offer a solution. In fact, the new approach may negate existing strengths that may lead some students to achieve learning successes. As well, the new approach may ignore the real instructional issues that may impede student success.

Second, often, the search for solutions is driven by "what works" on average (Bryk et al., 2015, p. 35). Districts adopt programs and approaches because studies found a statistically significant improvement in certain specific variables with certain specific samples of students. The pursuit of what works on average may ignore the variation in strengths, needs, and contexts across schools, classrooms, and students. Leaders must understand and appreciate the variation in strengths, needs, and contexts in order to determine how to best support educators in getting the most from any instructional practice in ways that will increase student success.

Relatedly, leaders must develop deep understanding of the systems that influence current outcomes (Bryk et al., 2015). Leadership teams should appreciate that the teachers they support did not hire themselves, they did not teach themselves to become educators, they did not evaluate themselves throughout their careers, and in general, they did not plan and implement their own professional development. The effectiveness of initial instruction is influenced greatly by the systems that leaders have perpetuated. If leadership teams fail to understand those systems and understand how to best refine, complement, or re-invent those systems, it may be unlikely that any improvement effort will achieve its potential.

Table 5.1 Challenges and Rewards of Promoting Effective Initial Instruction

| Issue | The Challenges | The Rewards |
|---|---|---|
| **Focusing on improvements to initial instruction that matter for all, but especially for groups who have experienced minimal academic success** | Leadership teams should acknowledge that materials, programs, and approaches should only be considered tools with limited inherent value. Real changes in outcomes (especially for groups who have been underserved) depend upon the team's ability to build the capacity of educators to use tools well, so that all students can demonstrate academic success. | By focusing on a few core instructional issues that matter most, leadership teams can build a school's positive transformational culture and strengthen the sense of collective efficacy. |
| **Focusing on a few key school-wide instructional improvements for extended time periods** | Leadership teams need to avoid quick solutions that promise great results based upon statistically significant controlled research study outcomes. Instead, teams should focus on determining which core instructional practices could elevate learning outcomes, especially for students who have been underserved. Educators are most likely to become proficient with new practices when they have the benefit to learn as a team over extended periods of time. | When schools stop chasing education's pendulum and persistently focus on a few powerful instructional practices that build upon the strengths and address the needs of their students, improvements in learning outcomes become likely. |

*(Continued)*

Table 5.1 (Continued)

| Issue | The Challenges | The Rewards |
|---|---|---|
| **Helping educators appreciate the value of the desired instructional improvements** | Leadership teams should know that powerful improvements in initial instruction are not likely to be achieved or sustained if educators do not understand, believe in, and appreciate the changes they are asked to pursue. | When educators know leaders respect their perspectives, input, and engagement, educators are more likely to work in ways that generate the greatest results from instructional improvements. |
| **Helping educators believe they have abundant time and support to learn to implement instructional improvements well** | Leaders should understand and appreciate how systems have influenced the teaching practices that generate current learning results. As well, leaders must understand and appreciate how they need to develop new systems or modify old systems in ways that will support teachers in mastering more effective practices. Leading a critical mass of teachers to master effective instructional practices requires a substantial investment of time and support. | When educators believe their leaders and colleagues are committed to helping them implement new practices in ways that will generate improved outcomes for all student groups, educators are more likely to experience a positive transformational culture, and the sense of collective efficacy will grow. |

Effective Initial Instruction

# Effective Initial Instruction: What It Is and What It Isn't

**(X) What It Isn't: Embracing Practices or Programs That Have Demonstrated Statistically Significant Outcomes in Controlled Studies**

> While rigorous studies of educational practices and programs often have merit, statistical outcomes reflect averages and may not shed adequate light on the complexities of various contexts that might influence educational outcomes. Specific practices and programs may or may not be powerful enough to promote the learning outcomes needed for populations of students within a school or district. In fact, many practices or programs with a substantial base of evidence may not be designed to generate the learning outcomes your school hopes to achieve.

**(✓) What It Is: Identifying, Focusing Upon, and Committing to Instructional Improvements That Have a Strong Likelihood of Building Upon the Strengths of Your Students and Educators**

> In NCUST award-winning schools, educators improved learning outcomes for all their students by focusing on improving a few powerful instructional practices that could advance student learning across multiple courses, disciplines, and grade levels. Educators implemented and refined the practices with specific goals in mind (e.g., increasing students' sense of belonging, building students' understanding of complex concepts, increasing student engagement). Implementation of the practice was not the goal. Instead, the practice was an important means to pursue the goal of improving learning outcomes.

**(X) What It Isn't: Finding a Quick Fix to Elevate Learning Outcomes**

> If quick fixes work at all, they usually don't work for long. The perennial search for "canned" solutions demoralizes committed educators, especially when the practices and programs

promoted offer teachers minimal opportunities to utilize their knowledge, perspectives, and commitment in ways that can enhance learning outcomes for students.

### ✓ What It Is: Focusing on the Long-Term Improvement of a Few Critical Teaching Practices

In order to generate and sustain strong improvements in learning outcomes for all students, leadership teams need to focus on long-term improvements to systems that influence how teachers provide initial instruction. In particular, leadership teams need to focus on creating systems that lead teachers to believe they have abundant high-quality support to make substantial improvements in initial instruction. Systems should lead teachers to believe leaders are committed to helping them successfully educate all their students.

### ✗ What It Isn't: Mandating Teacher Compliance

Mandates may change what teachers implement in classrooms; however, mandates rarely ensure quality implementation. If teachers believe they don't have the opportunity to learn about the practices under consideration, see the practices utilized with students who have similar strengths and needs as their students, see and discuss data about implementation, ask questions, and raise concerns, it is unlikely that any mandate will lead to high-quality implementation.

### ✓ What It Is: Helping Teachers Appreciate the Value of Desired Instructional Improvements

In NCUST award-winning schools, leadership teams lead educators to understand that the goal is not to generate compliance or to implement a practice specifically as defined in a teacher's manual or a script. Instead, leadership teams create an environment in which educators embrace the goal of generating substantially better learning outcomes for all their students. As well, leadership teams create an environment in which educators learn they can support each other in generating excellent outcomes for their students by helping each other use their knowledge, experience, and commitment as they implement an improvement effort.

### ⓧ What It Isn't: Paving the Route to Success With Evaluations

In some schools, teachers feel their implementation of a practice is evaluated before they understand the basic components of the practice or the rationale for the practice. In such schools, some educators are hesitant to try the components that are least comfortable for them because they don't want to receive a poor evaluation. In some schools, educators find ways to rebel in ways that result in the abandonment of improvement efforts that could have made a positive difference for students.

### ✓ What It Is: Paving the Route to Success With Support

In NCUST award-winning schools, teachers have reported that their leaders expect a lot; however, their leaders provide a quality and quantity of support that makes teachers believe they are likely to succeed. Leaders provide so many opportunities for educators to observe strong implementation, ask questions, receive guidance, attempt implementation, receive supportive feedback, try again, and receive even more supportive feedback that improvement becomes ubiquitous. The provision of such extensive support requires time. As well, the use of the time allotted is enhanced through structures that maximize collaborative learning and working.

## Tips for Leadership Teams

*How Schools Can Improve the Effectiveness of Initial Instruction (Remember to Review and Implement These Tips Regularly)*

- If your school has not yet identified one or two powerful teaching practices that could substantially increase the effectiveness of initial instruction, engage the leadership team in identifying practices that could accelerate the learning of your students. Engage the leadership team in studying *Teaching Practices from America's Best Urban Schools*. Study classrooms in your school where high percentages of students from all demographic groups exhibit outstanding learning results. Visit another school in your area where students from all demographic groups achieve outstanding learning results. Conduct empathy interviews with students (especially students from groups that historically have not been served well) to ask their perspectives about teaching practices that help them learn and teaching practices that make learning more difficult or less motivating. As a team, discuss how certain specific teaching practices might complement existing instructional improvement efforts within your school or district.

- Before deciding upon specific teaching practices to pursue, ensure that all members of the school team have excellent opportunities to participate in discussions about the practices, ask questions about their implementation, develop an understanding of why the practices positively influence student learning, and develop an understanding of the challenges associated with implementation.
- As a leadership team, resist the temptation to pursue the implementation of too many practices. Instead, select one, two, or three practices that have the highest likelihood of building on the school's strengths and addressing the learning needs of students (especially students who have historically not been served well). Select practices that could help improve learning outcomes throughout the school.
- As a leadership team, discuss the systems that have directly or indirectly reinforced teaching practices that conflict with the practices the team wishes to promote. Consider how previous professional development efforts, program adoptions, teacher observation or evaluation protocols, teacher collaboration routines, or other systems may need to be modified, minimized, refined, or abandoned in order to best support the implementation of the practices the team wishes to promote.
- As a leadership team, consider the development of a variety of supports that can help teachers develop skill in implementing the instructional practices the team wishes to promote. The team should consider strategies that will lead teachers to feel enthusiastic (not fearful) about

trying to implement the practices. The team should consider how they can create multiple opportunities over an extended period of time for teachers to continue to learn about the practices and to discuss their questions about the practices and the difficulties they experience in trying to implement the practices.

- The leadership team should work to create multiple opportunities for teachers to observe each other implementing the practices through affirming learning walks in which all feedback acknowledges and celebrates teachers' progress in implementing the practices and emphasizes the positive impact of the teaching practices on students' learning (Ross et al., 2023).

- As teachers become more confident in their implementation of the teaching practices, emphasis should be placed on establishing the school as a model for the implementation of the practice. The teaching practices pursued should be considered "signature practices" that benefit every student. Teacher progress in implementing the practices should be celebrated, and teachers should have abundant opportunities to learn from and emulate the most successful implementation efforts.

# Where Is Your School on the Road to Improving the Effectiveness of Initial Instruction?

The school leadership team should consider using the rubric in Table 5.2 to assess the school's progress toward improving the effectiveness of initial instruction. By reviewing the rubric each semester, the leadership team may identify and celebrate areas of growth and identify areas where additional growth is needed.

Table 5.2 Rubric for Assessing the School's Progress toward Improving the Effectiveness of Initial Instruction

| | Blazing New Paths of Equity/Excellence (Exemplary) | Entering a Whole New Environment (Approaching) | At Early Mile Markers (Developing) | At the Highway On-Ramp (Waiting) |
|---|---|---|---|---|
| Focusing on improvements to initial instruction that matter for all, but especially for groups who have experienced minimal academic success were expected to learn | Teachers demonstrate substantial progress in implementing the selected processes; however, teachers continue to strive for improved implementation that yields better learning outcomes for their students. | The leadership team has identified one, two, or at most three powerful teaching practices and has developed a set of supports that are likely to help teachers implement the practices well. Teachers are enthusiastically working to improve their use of the selected practices. | The leadership team has begun the process of identifying powerful teaching practices that could accelerate learning for many students. (See the first suggestion previously in Tips for Leadership Teams.) | There is no school-wide focus on efforts to improve initial instruction. Often, many students require intervention because initial instruction was ineffective. |
| Focusing on a few key school-wide instructional improvements for extended time periods | Even after one or two years of implementation, the leadership team continues to support teachers in improving implementation of the selected practices, unless there is substantial evidence of successful school-wide implementation. | When pressures emerge to shift the focus of instructional improvement efforts, leaders examine evidence to determine how well the school has implemented the current focus. Leaders resist efforts to change the focus prematurely. | The leadership team commits to focusing on the same few instructional improvements until high-quality implementation is achieved. | Instructional improvement initiatives change frequently without any evidence that implementation of a practice has improved. |

(Continued)

Table 5.2 (Continued)

| | Blazing New Paths of Equity/Excellence (Exemplary) | Entering a Whole New Environment (Approaching) | At Early Mile Markers (Developing) | At the Highway On-Ramp (Waiting) |
|---|---|---|---|---|
| Helping educators appreciate the value of the desired instructional improvements | Even when teachers achieve good measures of implementation of selected practices, teachers continue to push toward exemplary implementation because of the potential impact on students. | As areas of improvement are pursued, teachers feel valued and respected because dialogue is centered on both the efforts of teachers to implement the practices well and the impact on students. | As areas of focus for instructional improvement are considered and pursued, teachers perceive that their voices and perspectives are heard and valued. | Teachers do not perceive they have a voice in decisions about the focus of instructional improvement efforts. Their insights and perspectives are not heard. |
| Helping educators believe they have abundant time and support to learn to implement instructional improvements well | Even when teachers achieve good measures of implementation of selected practices, teachers benefit from supports that help them to become models for the implementation of the selected practices. | Teachers perceive they have abundant supports that enable them to learn about and become skillful in using the instructional practices the school is pursuing. | Leadership teams listen to teachers to determine the supports that teachers might need in order to implement instructional improvements well. Leadership teams work with teachers to put supports in place. | Teachers have a mandate to improve their implementation of instruction; however, they have few or no supports to help them improve. |

# References

Bryk, A. S., Gomez, L. M., Grunow, A., & LeMahieu, P. G. (2015). *Learning to improve: How America's schools can get better at getting better.* Cambridge, MA: Harvard Education Press.

Fullan, M. (2011). *Change leader: Learning to do what matters most.* San Francisco, CA: Jossey-Bass.

Hattie, J. (2023). *Visible learning: The sequel.* New York: Routledge and Taylor & Francis Group.

Hattie, J., & Zierer, K. (2018). *10 mindframes for visible learning: Teaching for success.* New York: Routledge and Taylor & Francis Group.

Johnson, J. F., Uline, C. L., & Munro, S. J. (2023). *When Black students excel: How schools can engage and empower Black students.* New York: Routledge and Taylor & Francis Group.

Johnson, J. F., Uline, C. L., & Perez, L. G. (2017). *Leadership in America's best urban schools.* New York: Routledge and Taylor & Francis Group.

Johnson, J. F., Uline, C. L., & Perez, L. G. (2019). *Teaching practices from America's Best Urban Schools: A guide for school and classroom leaders.* New York: Routledge and Taylor & Francis Group.

Ross, D. L., Lamb, L. L., & Johnson, J. F. (2023). Using affirming learning walks to build capacity. *Journal of School Administration Research and Development, 8*(1), 47–54.

Senge, P., Cambron-McCabe, N., Lucas, T., Smith, B., Dutton, J., & Kleiner, A. (2012). *Schools that learn: A fifth discipline fieldbook for educators, parents, and everyone who cares about education.* New York: Crown Business.

Theokas, C., González, M. L., Manriquez, C., & Johnson, J. F. (2019). *Five practices for improving the success of Latino students: A guide for secondary school leaders.* New York: Routledge and Taylor & Francis Group.

# Monitoring, Confirming, and Enhancing Learning

**Voices of Students and Parents From America's Best Schools**

"In classes at Hazard Elementary, you know exactly what your teachers want you to learn. It makes it easier to succeed, even when the stuff they want you to learn is hard."
– Maribel, fifth-grade student, R. F. Hazard Elementary, Garden Grove, California

"One of the things that helped me was one-on-one time with my teachers. My teachers would make sure I understood the material and helped me so my grades would go up. The dedicated teachers at Feaster Charter, the unwavering support of my family, and the caring staff all played a crucial role in shaping me into a well-rounded individual, helping me thrive socially, emotionally, and academically."
– Jessie, a high school student who attended Feaster Charter Middle in Chula Vista, California

"I love the way teachers at Hazard love to see you really understand things. If you don't get it the first time, they'll ask you questions and figure out that you don't get it. Then, they'll teach you, so you definitely get it! It's hard to not learn because the teachers want you to succeed."
– Ben, a fifth-grade student at R. F. Hazard Elementary, Garden Grove, California

> "If it weren't for my Feaster family, I would have been unable to reach my potential. Getting the help I needed made me realize I wanted to follow in my teachers' footsteps and help kids, too. After I graduated, I started taking Applied Behavior Analysis (ABA) courses and now I am a registered behavioral technician."
> – Gus, a graduate who attended Feaster Charter Middle in Chula Vista, California

## VIGNETTE K: Feaster Charter School, Chula Vista, California

**WON NCUST'S AMERICA'S BEST SCHOOL AWARD IN 2015 AND 2023**

*The streets near Feaster Charter School are lined with modest apartments, single-family homes, and trailer parks. Parents reported that the school's office staff always treated them as distinguished visitors, regardless of their residence or the language they speak at home. The welcoming environment is one part of the school's commitment to "foster the academic, social, emotional, and physical achievement of all students in school and in life." Building strong, positive relationships with the schools' 1,100 students, their families, and the community is considered a crucial first step.*

*Feaster educators recognize, however, that the first step can't be the only step. In particular, they believe they must find ways to ensure that Feaster students (including those who are multi-lingual learners and who meet low-income criteria) learn the challenging academic skills expected of all California students. Working as close-knit teams, Feaster educators plan and learn together to ensure students at each grade level learn challenging academic skills.*

*Feaster's grade-level teams don't shy away from the difficult learning expectations articulated in state standards. Instead, teachers embrace high expectations, assuming they will help each other lead students to success. For example, the sixth-grade team worked to ensure their students could cite textual evidence to support their analysis of a passage. To determine how well students were progressing toward this state-wide expectation, the students were asked to read a complex text and cite evidence that indicated why democracy was the best form of government. Students had been taught to use the restate, answer, cite, and explain (R.A.C.E.) strategy to develop a thorough and organized response. Teachers met to review and analyze the students' work. They critically examined the students' responses to learn what students did well and where students could do more to demonstrate proficiency with the objective. Teachers supported each other in identifying teaching strategies that could help students succeed with this challenging task. For example, they determined students might be more likely to produce outstanding work if the students referenced a reading annotation guide that teachers posted. As well, the teachers determined students were more likely to be successful if students read their responses to themselves before submission. This kind of thoughtful effort to enhance instruction has influenced improved learning outcomes for Feaster students over the past several years.*

*Throughout Feaster, teachers are constantly checking student progress by asking students thought-provoking questions, by facilitating academic small-group conversations, and by asking students to explain their work, often taking note of what students understand and what they are yet to understand. As well, Feaster students proudly track their progress toward mastering rigorous academic expectations. Feaster's students see evidence, in their own work, that they are on the path to success at school and in life.*

## VIGNETTE L: R. F. Hazard Elementary, Garden Grove, California

### WON NCUST'S AMERICA'S BEST SCHOOL AWARD IN 2020

*Before California adopted more challenging academic standards in 2010, leaders in the Garden Grove Unified School District recognized the importance of establishing systems to build the capacity of teachers to ensure all the district's students would meet the state's rigorous academic expectations. The new systems established instructional leadership teams that would build the capacity of teachers in each school to understand key standards and support each other in planning effective* instruction that would lead all students to learn the new standards well. In 2018, when Olivia Hufnagel became principal at R. F. Hazard Elementary, she assumed responsibility for refining the school-level systems that Hazard's team of veteran teachers had put into place.

Principal Hufnagel explained that Hazard teachers meet in vertical teams to provide school-wide leadership to improvement efforts. Vertical teams determine what students should learn before they leave sixth grade. Collaborative discussions build alignment between grade levels and promote rigor as students advance from one year to the next.

Additionally, teachers meet regularly as grade-level professional learning communities to determine what their students (at each grade level from transitional kindergarten to grade 6) should do to demonstrate they meet the expectations for their grade level. As well, grade-level teams meet weekly to collaboratively identify best teaching practices that can help ensure students meet grade-level expectations. The teacher teams support each other as they "start with the end in mind" and use data to drive their instructional planning. Specifically, Principal Hufnagel emphasized that teachers aim to see evidence that students are listening, speaking, reading, and writing in ways that demonstrate their understanding of important academic concepts and skills.

Hazard teachers and staff have established a culture of high expectations for what their students should learn and a shared sense of responsibility to support students in their educational journey. Additionally, teachers have developed common strategies to maximize the likelihood that all their students (90% of whom meet low-income criteria and almost 40% of whom are emerging as multi-lingual learners) will successfully meet high academic expectations. As students progress from one grade level to the next, the instructional strategies build in complexity so that upper-grade students are likely to engage successfully in complex listening, speaking, reading, and writing tasks, such as Socratic seminars.

Principal Hufnagel explained that learning at R. F. Hazard Elementary is driven by formative assessments and frequent checks for understanding designed to determine what students understand well and what support might help students understand better. She explained that teachers persistently check for understanding by listening to students' academic discourse, by analyzing what students write, or by looking carefully at end-of-lesson exit tickets. She said, "My teachers *are knowledgeable about their grade-level standards and have taught in various grade levels to understand well the vertical alignment of standards. They are thoughtful in their planning and use formative and summative assessments to drive teaching and learning. They build student agency through goal setting and reflections, but more importantly, they build a love of learning in all they do." As a result, success is not accidental. It is optimized.*

---

Marzano (2003, p. 23) distinguished the intended curriculum (the content specified by the state, district, or school) from the implemented curriculum (the content actually presented by the teacher) and the attained curriculum (the content learned by students). Chapter 4 emphasized the importance of ensuring that the implemented curriculum was rigorous (aligned to district, state, or professional standards) yet was also viable because teachers were likely to have sufficient time to teach well whichever concepts and skills they worked to have their students learn. Chapter 4 also emphasized the importance of guaranteeing all students benefit from the implemented curriculum by ensuring all educators who teach the same grade levels, or the same courses, teach their students the same rigorous content. As well, the implemented curriculum is guaranteed when teachers across grade levels collaborate to ensure smooth transitions through grade levels and course levels in ways that maximize students' ongoing academic success.

Then, Chapter 5 described how leadership teams worked together to help ensure all educators provided effective initial instruction that resulted in all student groups learning the implemented curriculum well. The energy from the rigorous curricula gear ignited the effective initial instruction gear in a way that prompted educators to consider, "If these are the concepts and skills we believe all students must learn, how can we support each other in designing learning environments and shaping initial learning opportunities in ways that help all our students succeed?" With effective initial instruction, schools begin to ensure that the implemented curriculum becomes the curriculum attained (learned) by all student groups.

In Chapter 6, we describe how leadership teams in NCUST award-winning schools monitor, confirm, and enhance learning in ways that further maximize the likelihood that the implemented curriculum (the concepts and skills teachers endeavor to teach) becomes the attained curriculum (the concepts and skills students actually learn). In NCUST award-winning schools, the energy from the rigorous curricula gear and the effective initial instruction gear combine to inspire a school-wide urgency to determine, "How can we be certain all our students are progressing toward mastery of the important concepts and skills we endeavored to teach today, this week, or this month? How can we confirm that our initial instruction truly was effective for each of our students? Did our students learn what we endeavored to teach? What did they understand? What did they not understand? What misconceptions might have interfered with understanding? How can we build upon what students understood well? Which students mastered the concepts and skills? Which students did not? How can we help more students achieve mastery so that our implemented curriculum becomes the students' acquired curriculum?"

The image on the left side of Figure 6.1 illustrates the relationship between the intended curriculum, the implemented curriculum, and the attained curriculum in many typical schools throughout the United States. The image on the right side illustrates the relationship between the intended, implemented, and attained curriculum in most NCUST award-winning schools.

Generally, state and local education agencies expect leaders at all schools in their jurisdictions (including NCUST award-winning schools) to implement the state's or district's intended curriculum. So, in Figure 6.1 the intended curriculum is similarly sized for both typical schools and NCUST award-winning schools.

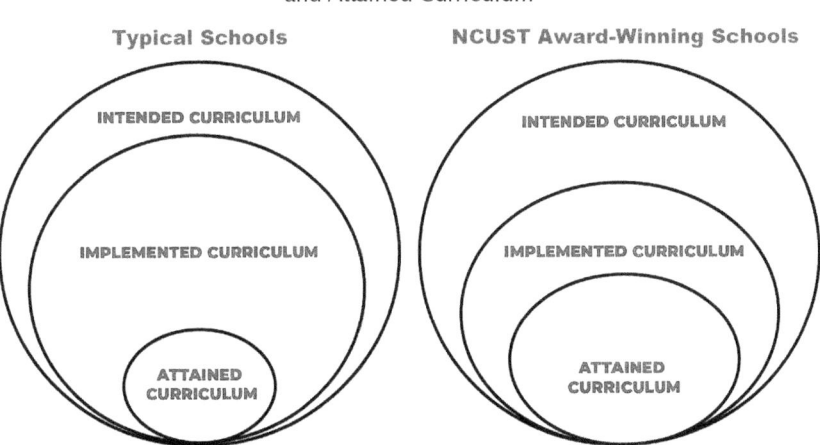

*Figure 6.1* Relationship Between the Intended, Implemented, and Attained Curriculum

Often, as discussed in Chapter 4, leaders at NCUST award-winning schools find ways to help educators implement a more viable curriculum that prioritizes the most important, rigorous concepts and skills. In contrast, educators at more typical schools might feel compelled to cover all state standards or implement a textbook completely. So, in Figure 6.1, the implemented curriculum in typical schools is shown as larger than the implemented curriculum in NCUST award-winning schools.

The greatest difference, however, is often in the attained curriculum. In Figure 6.1, the attained curriculum is larger for NCUST award-winning schools than for typical schools. Students at NCUST award-winning schools generally demonstrate more evidence that they have learned more (and more rigorous) concepts and skills than their counterparts statewide or districtwide. For example, even though over 80% of students at Feaster Charter School (Vignette I) met low-income criteria and over 50% were emerging as multi-lingual learners, greater percentages of Feaster's seventh- and eighth-grade students met or exceeded California standards in English language arts (based on the 2023 state assessment) than did seventh- and eighth-grade students throughout California. Similarly, even though over 90% of students at R.F. Hazard Elementary (Vignette J) met low-income criteria and 40% were emerging as multi-lingual learners, greater percentages of Hazard's students met or exceeded California standards in English language arts and mathematics (based on the 2023 state assessment) than did elementary students throughout California.

Chapter 5 ("Effective Initial Instruction") and Chapter 6 ("Monitoring, Confirming, and Enhancing Learning") help explain why a smaller implemented curriculum can result in a larger attained curriculum for all student groups. When leadership teams make deliberate, sustained, school-wide efforts to ensure that student learning of rigorous curricula is regularly and consistently monitored, confirmed, and enhanced, teaching less can result in students learning more. Leadership teams play a critical role in ensuring that learning is regularly and consistently monitored, confirmed, and enhanced.

## What Leadership Teams Accomplished to Monitor, Confirm, and Enhance Learning

Wiggins and McTighe (2005) encouraged educators to start with the "end in mind" as a means to help students learn rigorous concepts and skills.

Educators may be tempted to rush to identify interesting lesson activities, relevant readings, or appropriate experiments related to a topic; however, the wiser approach to lesson planning first considers what students are meant to learn and second what constitutes evidence that students have learned the desired content. As described in Chapter 4, typically educators in NCUST award-winning schools start with the end in mind by working together to specify what they want students to learn. However, this agreed-upon "end" might never become the attained curriculum without deliberate attention to monitoring, confirming, and enhancing learning.

To help ensure all student groups were likely to learn the school's rigorous curricula, leadership teams developed common strategies to monitor, confirm, and enhance student learning. Specifically, leadership teams developed, adopted, or adapted formative assessment tools that were used in a consistent manner across grade levels or courses to determine what concepts and skills students had or had not learned. The tools were used systematically to inform how teachers might refine instruction and enhance student learning. Leadership teams put systems in place to ensure students and their parents benefited from unambiguous feedback about the learning progress students were making. Beyond the systematic use of periodic formative assessments, leadership teams supported teachers in creating and implementing strategies to acquire immediate feedback about the extent to which students were understanding the concepts and skills taught during each lesson.

## *Leadership Teams Developed/Adopted/Adapted Formative Assessments That Align Specifically to the Concepts and Skills Students are Expected to Learn*

Unfortunately, in most schools in the U.S., assessments are not used in ways that enhance student learning. Stiggins explained:

> Assessment is the process of gathering evidence of student learning to inform educational decisions. Student success hinges on the quality of those decisions, and the quality of those decisions depends on the quality of the evidence (assessment results) upon which they are based. U.S. students are at risk because our national, state, local district, school, and classroom assessment systems very often do not

yield the kinds of evidence required for sound instructional decision making where it really matters: in the classroom. Typically, these systems provide only gross indicators of student achievement that cannot inform the classroom-level instructional decisions that truly drive school quality.

(2017, p. 5)

In most schools throughout the U.S., teachers believe they are teaching students academic standards. However, in many schools, the primary tools educators use to know how well their students have learned academic standards are annual state assessment reports. Those reports often arrive too late and with insufficient detail to influence classroom instruction.

Many districts have tried to supplement annual state assessments with benchmark assessments administered two, three, or four times a year. Leadership teams in some NCUST award-winning schools have become excellent consumers of benchmark assessment data because they promptly receive and analyze information that conveys how well students mastered the specific concepts and skills teachers endeavored to teach. However, many teachers and administrators do not receive adequate, timely, actionable information from benchmark assessments to determine: (1) Which concepts and skills did my students master? (2) Did my students demonstrate mastery of the concepts and skills I thought I already taught? (3) How might I refine my instructional plans for the next nine weeks? More typically, if principals and teachers learn anything from benchmark assessments, they learn what percentage of their students appear to be on track for demonstrating proficiency on the end-of-year assessment. However, most teachers and administrators do not know which standards or objectives their students have learned and which have not been learned. Most educators cannot say how the data will influence how they will adapt their instruction to meet their students' needs. In some schools, educators will know which students will receive extra support in response to the benchmark assessment results. Still, in most schools, it is rare to find that the extra support is focused on specific concepts and skills the students need to learn.

Classroom assessments can be better tools for monitoring, confirming, and enhancing learning; however, in many schools, classroom assessments provide little information about the specific concepts and skills students understand. For example, in a struggling school, we asked a fourth-grade teacher how she knew if her students understood the concepts she had been teaching regarding place value and rounding whole numbers. The teacher shared a teacher-made assessment with 20 items. The teacher proudly indicated that many of her students had achieved mastery because they correctly answered 80% or more of the items. A closer look at the assessment revealed that five of the multiple-choice items on the assessment reviewed a previously taught geometry objective. Eight of the remaining ten multiple-choice items did not include distractors that required students to make more challenging decisions about rounding (e.g., Round 3,520 to the nearest hundred: Choose either A-6,200, B-300, C-3,500, D-20). There were another five items that required students to round multi-digit numbers to the hundreds, thousands, or ten thousands place (without choices or additional prompts).

A quick glance at the student work revealed that many of the students who answered 80% or more correctly answered all five of the geometry review items and all eight of the easier multiple-choice items correctly. However, several of the students who achieved an 80% score answered only three or four of the remaining seven items. Did those students truly understand place value and rounding? Would they be able to apply the concepts they understood to solve more challenging rounding problems? It is certainly important to know that students retained knowledge of concepts previously learned. As well, it is important to know that students could correctly answer easier multiple-choice items. However, those successes should not obscure the possibility that learning could be enhanced for some students to help them acquire a deeper conceptual understanding of rounding and place value.

In NCUST award-winning schools (such as Feaster Charter School: Vignette I and Hazard Elementary: Vignette J), teachers who teach the same grade or the same course generally agree on how they will assess student learning before they begin teaching the concept or skill. In some cases, they adopt publisher-developed tools. At times, they adapt tools to better align to the specific objectives teachers want their students to learn. In other cases, teachers work together to create their own assessment tools using item banks or items they create that align well with their learning intentions.

Typically, the formative assessments are specific and challenging enough to provide teachers a more complete assessment of what students have learned and what they are yet to learn. In NCUST award-winning schools, we have heard many teachers say, "When our students perform well on our assessment, they perform well on the annual state assessment because we made sure ours is more rigorous." As well, we've heard teachers say, "If our students perform well on our assessment, we know they will perform well at the next grade level or in the next course." The assessment strategy may or may not include multiple-choice items. It may or may not resemble a state assessment. The assessment strategy may not include paper/pencil assessment at all. In general, however, in NCUST award-winning schools, teachers agree upon a tool that allows them to monitor and confirm the extent to which students have learned the concepts and skills they endeavor to teach.

In NCUST award-winning schools, the assessments adopted, adapted, or created by teachers are designed to give teachers information they can use to improve instruction. Teachers understand the rationale behind each assessment item. They know what each task will tell them about what their students understand. Teachers know how to look at student work and identify possible misconceptions. One teacher explained, "Sometimes my students get the correct answer for the wrong reason. That's why I ask them to show their work. I'm trying to teach them to think." Often, teachers design assessments strategically so they will know how to use the assessment results to determine how instruction for some students might need to be enhanced. DuFour and Marzano (2011) explained that effective collaborative teams planned and utilized formative assessment primarily to improve learning results. To improve learning results, formative assessments must provide teachers useful information about each student's understanding of a specific concept or skill.

For example, the sixth-grade team at Feaster Charter School (Vignette I) came together to review their students' writing not only because they wanted to monitor how well their students could cite textual evidence to support their analysis of a passage but also because they wanted to determine how they could refine instructional strategies in ways that led more of their students to master the objective. The teachers administered the same assessment during the same time frame. Together, they reviewed the student work to determine what their students were doing well and how they needed to improve. Also, in an objective and supportive manner, the teachers identified practical ways they could enhance instruction over the next few days so they could increase the likelihood that all their students would demonstrate mastery of this literacy skill.

Unfortunately, the strategic use of assessments as a tool to improve instruction is rare in most U.S. schools. Assessment in typical schools (especially typical secondary schools) is an end-of-the-road event, for example, end of the unit, end of the chapter, end of the month, end of the semester. In many typical schools, teachers administer and grade assessments, record scores in their grade book, and move on to a different topic. In contrast, teachers in most NCUST award-winning schools develop and administer truly formative assessments, designed to help them "form" instruction that builds upon what their students demonstrated they have already learned and best addresses what their students demonstrated they still need to learn. Teachers at Hazard Elementary (Vignette J) established a variety of formative strategies for determining what students understood and did not understand.

Figure 1.1 shows that the monitoring, confirming, and enhancing learning gear should influence the transfer of energy and power to the intervention and enrichment gear. This does not occur accidentally. It only happens when teachers use the results of common formative assessments to determine how they will enhance instruction in ways that lead more of their students to gain deeper understandings of challenging concepts and skills.

## *Leadership Teams Developed and Refined Daily Teaching Practices That Help Monitor, Confirm, and Enhance the Learning of Important Concepts and Skills*

By helping teachers adopt, adapt, or create common formative assessments, leadership teams help educators start with the end in mind and enable their colleagues to better monitor, confirm, and enhance learning. Simultaneously, leadership teams support educators in establishing day-to-day, lesson-to-lesson, and even minute-to-minute strategies for monitoring, confirming, and enhancing the learning of important concepts and skills. In NCUST award-winning schools, educators do not wait until they administer a common formative assessment to determine if students can explain key concepts, apply important skills, or model key relationships. Instead, educators proactively use multiple strategies to acquire evidence of student understanding. Leadership teams support educators in considering options for determining that students are generating meaning from texts, building understanding from conversations, making sense of processes, and progressing toward deep understanding and mastery of important concepts and skills.

In many NCUST award-winning schools, we have observed leadership team members working with their colleagues to help them specify the concepts students will need to understand in order to demonstrate the learning outcomes associated with complex standards. Without such support, novice educators might approach a standard as something to be learned in one step. Often teacher leaders help their colleagues "break down" standards to determine what students will need to understand so they can demonstrate mastery.

For example, in a math class in a typical high school, a teacher may plan to teach her students how functions model the relationship between two sets of numbers. When the teacher notices that the textbook dedicates four pages to functions, she may plan to address the first page on Monday and each of the next three pages on the following three days. The teacher may assume her students will be ready to take the department's common formative assessment on Friday. Many math teachers today might have learned to correctly calculate answers to questions about mathematical functions with the help of four pages from a similar textbook. Standards today, however, require students to do more than correctly calculate answers about algebraic functions. Instead, students must be able to demonstrate deeper levels of understanding.

In contrast, at an NCUST award-winning school, a member of the school's leadership team might facilitate a discussion that pushes her colleagues to consider what students need to understand to be able to explain how real phenomena (especially things relevant to teenagers) might appear in a two-column table. As well, teachers might be asked to consider what students would need to understand to show how the data from the table could be communicated on a coordinate plane. Additionally, teachers might be asked to think about what students would need to know to be able to use data from the table and/or from the coordinate plane to develop a mathematical expression that described the relationship between the two columns of data. As well, teachers might want to ensure students could talk about the mathematical expression in ways that related back to the data in the two-column table. Finally, teachers might want to learn if students understood the definition of a mathematical function sufficiently to determine if the relationship between the two columns of data could be considered a function. Throughout the discussion, emphasis would be placed on what teachers needed to see or hear to have reasonable certainty that students were developing a deep understanding of the concepts.

After teachers deconstruct the standard, teachers may decide that the four pages in the textbook are woefully inadequate to prepare their students to demonstrate the required level of understanding. Teachers may determine they will need significantly more time (beyond four days) to build the depth of understanding their students need. Most importantly, however, teachers will begin to determine what they need to see or hear from each student to monitor and confirm that students understand critical concepts.

In NCUST award-winning schools, continuous checking for understanding is not a routine for satisfying classroom observers. It is the expression of a commitment to monitor and confirm that each student is actively constructing strong understandings of the concepts and skills students need to learn. It is the acknowledgment that the information acquired from checking for understanding provides immediate opportunities to refine instruction and enhance learning so each student is more likely to acquire deep understanding of rigorous concepts (Fisher & Frey, 2007; Johnson, Uline, & Perez, 2019).

Teachers may use a wide array of strategies to monitor their students' understandings (e.g., small-group discussions, Socratic seminars, student use of individual whiteboards, exit tickets, total physical response activities, think-pair-share activities, hand signals, graphic organizers, randomized individual questioning, project-based activities); however, the strategy may not be as important as the goal. To maximize the likelihood of student success, the goal of checking understanding should be to monitor the extent to which each student is understanding the concepts and skills that are essential to building mastery. As well, the goal of checking understanding should be to acquire information that enables the teacher to refine instruction and enhance learning for each student served.

Figure 1.1 shows that the monitoring, confirming, and enhancing learning gear should influence the transfer of energy and power to the effective initial instruction gear. This does not occur accidentally. It happens when teachers use the development of a common formative assessment to spur their collaboration regarding strategies for checking to ensure that, each day in each lesson, students are making progress toward developing the building blocks that will lead them to mastery of challenging concepts and skills.

## Leadership Teams Ensured That the Information Acquired From Monitoring and Confirming Learning Is Communicated Effectively to Students and Family Members

In most typical schools, students are aware of which tasks they completed and how those tasks were scored or evaluated; however, students often have little awareness of which concepts and skills they have learned well and which they have not yet learned. Often, students assume accountability for completing tasks but may not realize that the real goal is to help them develop solid understandings.

In NCUST award-winning schools, often students know, up front and as they progress, the major concepts and skills they are expected to demonstrate by the end of the semester or the end of the school year. Often, students are able to explain, "These are the literacy skills I have already demonstrated this year and these are the skills I'm working to develop." Students demonstrated a sense of agency and ownership because they understood what they needed to learn. For example, at Feaster Charter School (Vignette I), students used data trackers and goal-setting processes to take ownership of their progress. At Wynnebrook Elementary (Vignette G), students understood what they needed to learn in order to advance literacy levels. At YMLA (Vignette B), students used district-developed software to keep track of the learning goals they achieved. Hattie (2023) found a 1.33 effect size in his meta-analysis of studies that explored the relationship between student ownership of their data and student achievement.

Often, in NCUST award-winning schools, information about the concepts and skills students have learned is integrated into electronic systems that allow parents to monitor their child's academic progress. In interviews with NCUST teams, parents shared how they use the school's electronic applications to discover what their child has learned well and what their child will be learning in the coming weeks. Some parents appreciated the opportunity to support and/or reinforce their child's learning. Consistently, parents expressed hopefulness because they recognized their children were demonstrating understanding of important academic skills. Parents were eager to support teachers and administrators because parents believed that school personnel were establishing real opportunities for their children to succeed in life.

## Why Monitoring, Confirming, and Enhancing Learning Is Challenging Yet Rewarding

Monitoring, confirming, and enhancing learning is much more challenging than following a scope and sequence chart, assigning pages from a workbook, following a scripted curriculum, or relying upon a software program. To monitor and confirm learning, educators need clarity about what learning needs to be monitored and how learning might be confirmed. To enhance learning, educators need practice at using formative strategies to determine how instruction might be refined in ways that advance and deepen understanding. In many schools, teachers are expected to monitor completion of tasks, not to monitor student-learning progress. They are expected to confirm scores and grade averages, not to confirm students' understanding of concepts. They are expected to end a unit on time, as specified by a curriculum calendar, not to enhance learning based on data from formative assessments. At many schools, monitoring, confirming, and enhancing *learning* represents a major shift in how educators approach their responsibilities.

NCUST award-winning schools have addressed this shift primarily by organizing time in ways that help teachers work in teams to help each other monitor, confirm, and enhance learning. Effective teamwork requires skillful leadership that establishes a safe, trusting environment and builds a positive transformational culture for educators. How many schools initiated professional learning communities, only to abandon the efforts because teachers felt they were treated "unprofessionally," educators perceived they weren't "learning" anything that helped them better serve their students, and a sense of "community" never emerged?

While it is easy to understand why it is difficult to build systems that monitor, confirm, and enhance learning, educators from NCUST award-winning schools eagerly explained why their efforts have been worthwhile. One educator made clear, "At first we met because we had to meet. Now, we meet because we fuel each other. We help each other think, plan, and grow. I can't imagine teaching without my team" (Johnson et al., 2019, p. 27).

Table 6.1 describes both the challenges and rewards of monitoring, confirming, and enhancing learning. However, the challenges and rewards might best be summarized in the story of Brazosport High School in Texas, a school that in the 1990s had a dismal record of academic success until the principal and his leadership team generated dramatic improvements in learning and earned an exemplary rating in the Texas accountability system. When a researcher asked the principal to describe the "bottom-line" differences between how the school operated previously (when achievement results were low) and how the school operated after multiple school-wide changes had been implemented and refined, the principal replied, "Well, back then, we taught school like we were feeding the chickens." When the interviewer asked for clarification, the principal offered the following explanation:

> When you feed the chickens, you strap on your bag of feed and go out into the yard and toss the feed onto the ground. If the chickens eat the feed, that's fine. If they don't, that's fine. Your job is just to toss it out there. That's the way we taught school. We strapped on our lesson plans, we went into our classrooms, and we tossed out the information. If the students got it, fine. If the students didn't get it, fine. Back then, we thought our job was just to present the information, to toss it out there. The difference now is that our teachers want to see evidence that students have taken it in, ingested it, and digested the information. We don't stop until we see evidence that students have understood what we want them to learn. That's the main difference between our school back then and our school today.
> (Johnson et al., 2019, p. 31)

For years, many public schools have "tossed out" information and hoped the students could acquire, internalize, and make sense of the information in ways that allowed them to succeed in postsecondary education, careers, and in their communities. Typically, schools have neither monitored nor confirmed that students were learning the important concepts and skills that influence their ability to succeed. Generally, when schools have noticed some students "look thin" because they have not learned important concepts and skills, educators have not received support that helped them enhance and improve their teaching in response to the student data acquired through monitoring efforts. Changing these systemic habits is not easy. However, the story of Brazosport High School, as well as the stories of many NCUST award-winning schools, illustrates that leadership teams can help schools change systemic habits in ways that generate impressive learning outcomes for all groups of students.

Table 6.1 Challenges and Rewards of Monitoring, Confirming, and Enhancing Learning

| Issue | The Challenges | The Rewards |
|---|---|---|
| Developing/adopting/adapting formative assessments that align specifically to the concepts and skills students are expected to learn | The development of common formative assessments requires planning from the teachers who share responsibility for teaching the content. Planning requires time as well as leadership support. Teachers may need access to item banks, project-based tasks, or other tools to help them make substantive decisions about items to include. Also, time needs to be set aside for teachers to work together to examine student work and determine implications for improving instruction. | When educators focus on monitoring and confirming student learning of essential concepts and skills, teachers are more likely to appreciate the potential power of the instruction they provide. They are more likely to find ways to enhance their students' learning. |
| Developing/adopting/adapting formative assessments that align specifically to the concepts and skills students are expected to learn | The proper use of common formative assessments requires educators to see assessments as mid-points rather than ending places. This paradigm shift is important in helping teachers ask, "What does this assessment tell me about what my students still need to learn?" and "How can I still improve instruction so my students' learning is enhanced?" | When educators start to see assessments as mid-points (not ending places), the school truly becomes a learning organization where teaching and learning improve continuously (Senge et al., 2012). In particular, intervention and enrichment become more effective in helping students achieve mastery. |

(Continued)

Table 6.1 (Continued)

| Issue | The Challenges | The Rewards |
|---|---|---|
| **Developing and refining daily teaching practices that help monitor, confirm, and enhance the learning of important concepts and skills.** | Many academic standards require students to develop deep understandings of concepts. Teachers need ongoing support in "unpacking" standards to identify the building blocks that can help students acquire and demonstrate understanding. As well, teachers need support in developing teaching practices that help them continuously monitor student learning of the building blocks. Many teachers may recognize that "chicken feeding" is not an effective strategy for many students; however, many teachers need ongoing support if they are to master new strategies. | Visitors to NCUST award-winning schools will ask, "How did they hire such amazing teachers?" The answer is often, they didn't hire them, they grew them. Leadership teams grow great teachers when they help teachers learn how to unpack and teach challenging standards. In particular, initial instruction becomes more effective in helping students achieve mastery. |
| **Ensuring that the information acquired from monitoring and confirming learning is communicated effectively to students and family members.** | Most teachers are accustomed to giving students and parents information used to calculate grades; however, often the information does not highlight what students have learned or what they are yet to learn. Often information about the concepts and skills students have learned is not communicated well to students or their family members. | When students see clearly what educators want them to learn, many students will surprise us by demonstrating their capacity to advance their learning. Similarly, when parents see clearly that their children are learning challenging content, many parents will surprise us by showing their willingness to support our efforts. |

# Monitoring, Confirming, and Enhancing Learning: What It Is and What It Isn't

### ✗ What It Isn't: Monitoring and Confirming Assignment/Test Completion

In many schools, educators monitor and confirm student completion of assignments and tests. As well, schools tend to monitor the scores and grades students earn. Often, however, the information acquired does not indicate what specific concepts and skills students learned or did not learn. At times, even when students earn good grades, there may be little evidence to confirm that students have learned the concepts and skills they need to succeed in school or in life.

### ✓ What It Is: Monitoring/Confirming Students Have Learned Important Concepts and Skills

In NCUST award-winning schools, educators agree upon the concepts and skills their students should learn at each grade and in each course. Furthermore, they agree upon what they should accept as evidence that students have learned those concepts well. Educators share a commitment to monitor each student's progress and confirm each student's mastery.

### ✗ What It Isn't: More Testing

In many schools, students would benefit from far less testing. In particular, students would benefit (and educators would benefit) from a dramatic reduction in testing that does not influence improvements in teaching and learning. Common formative assessments should not add to the quantity of testing in schools. Instead, common formative assessments should replace many tests and increase the likelihood that each assessment will lead to improved teaching and enhanced student learning.

## ✅ What It Is: Better and More Meaningful Assessment

In NCUST award-winning schools, educators use assessment not as an end to instruction but as part of an instructional process. Outstanding educators structure each assessment and the way each assessment is used to maximize the likelihood that the assessment results will help educators better understand what students have learned and what students haven't learned well. High quality assessment information helps teachers refine their strategies and enhance learning for each student.

## ❌ What It Isn't: Monitoring/Confirming Learning Only on "Assessment Days"

In some schools, teachers believe they monitor and confirm learning only on days when they administer formal assessments. When they present information, explain ideas, or model processes, they do not believe they need to focus on monitoring student understanding.

## ✅ What It Is: Continuous Monitoring/Confirming Learning as Part of Teaching

In NCUST award-winning schools, while educators are presenting, explaining, or modeling, they are constantly checking to determine if their students are understanding, making sense of the information, recognizing important distinctions, or making connections to their prior knowledge. In the instructional moment, outstanding educators need to know, "Is this making sense to each of my students?" So, interspersed throughout their teaching, educators ask students to explain; to demonstrate; to teach the concept to the student next to them; to draw and share a diagram that shows they understand the relationship between two concepts; to find, read, and explain evidence to support their claim; to describe why something makes sense; or to state why something doesn't make sense to them yet. Outstanding educators are always monitoring and confirming that students are making progress toward developing deep understandings.

### (X) What It Isn't: Sharing Assignments Completed and Scores Earned With Students and Parents

In many schools, educators share with students and parents information about student completion of assignments and the scores students earn on assignments and tests. This information may increase the likelihood that assignments are completed and that students earn better grades; however, it does not necessarily improve student mastery of important concepts and skills.

### (✓) What It Is: Sharing Information About Student Progress in Learning Important Concepts and Skills

In NCUST award-winning schools, educators ensure that students and their parents have information about the concepts and skills students are expected to learn. As well, students and their parents are kept abreast of the progress students are making in demonstrating understanding of those important concepts and skills. As a result, students and their parents are more likely to feel like partners in teaching/learning processes. Often, students express enthusiasm and pride regarding their progress learning challenging academic skills.

# Tips for Leadership Teams

*How Schools Can Improve the Monitoring, Confirming, and Enhancing of Learning (Remember to Review and Implement These Tips Regularly)*

- If your school has not yet identified the important concepts and skills all students should master (for each grade level or each course), you are encouraged to go back to Chapter 4 and address the tips for leadership teams focused upon rigorous curricula.

- If your school has identified the important concepts and skills all students should master (for each grade level or each course), arrange opportunities for colleagues to engage in deep discussions about how your students should demonstrate their mastery of the concept or skill. Through these collaborative conversations, generate consensus about your learning expectations for students.

- As a grade-level team, a course-alike team, or a department, select one important concept/skill to be learned by your students and develop an assessment that all team members will use to determine the extent to which each student has mastered the concept/skill. Aim to create an assessment that will be challenging enough to allow students to demonstrate deep understanding of the rigorous concepts you want your students to master. Remember that sometimes the best assessments are not paper-and-pencil tests. The best assessments should provide a window through which you can ascertain what your students understand, what they don't understand yet, and the issues that might be interfering with their understanding. Some teams start by aiming to create only a few common formative assessments the first year.

- After the first common formative assessment is developed and before instruction begins, work with colleagues to identify the "building blocks" that might help students develop the levels of understanding necessary to perform well on the common formative assessment. Define which concepts, ideas, distinctions, nuances, and so on might help your students develop a strong understanding. Determine questions you might ask students to discuss, writing tasks you might ask students to complete, small projects you might ask students to pursue, exit tickets you could use to conclude daily lessons, or other strategies that would help you teach the "building blocks" and simultaneously help you understand the extent to which your students are developing strong understandings.

- Agree upon a date (or a narrow window of dates) when the first common assessment will be administered by all members of the team. Also, agree upon a date and time when the team will convene and work together to review the students' work products, determine which students demonstrated mastery, which students did not, and what instructional enhancements might help students progress toward mastery.

- Create ways to communicate to your students and their parents about the concepts and skills they will learn. In addition to listing the concept/skill, provide an example of the kind of questions students will be able to answer when they've achieved mastery. Let students and parents know the dates planned for common formative assessments. Also, consider adding ideas for things students could do (and parents could do to help their children) in preparation. Be sure to let students and parents know how progress toward mastery will be factored into your grading.

# Where Is Your School on the Road to Monitoring, Confirming, and Enhancing Learning Results?

The school leadership team should consider using the rubric in Table 6.2 to assess the school's progress toward monitoring, confirming, and enhancing learning results. By reviewing the rubric each semester, the leadership team may identify and celebrate areas of growth and identify areas where additional growth is needed.

Table 6.2 Rubric for Assessing the School's Progress with Monitoring, Confirming, and Enhancing Learning Results

| | Blazing New Paths of Equity/Excellence (Exemplary) | Entering a Whole New Environment (Approaching) | At Early Mile Markers (Developing) | At the Highway On-Ramp (Waiting) |
|---|---|---|---|---|
| Developing, adopting, adapting formative assessments that align specifically to the concepts and skills students were expected to learn | As teams use common formative assessments, they constantly look for ways to improve the tools so they better align to rigorous learning expectations, monitor student learning, and confirm mastery. Over time, common formative assessments become better tools. | Each team of teachers in core subject areas regularly develops, adopts, or adapts common formative assessments that help shape the focus of teaching and learning for all students. | Each team of teachers in core subject areas has at least one common formative assessment they will use to monitor and confirm student progress. | Teams of teachers do not have common formative assessments that enable them to monitor or confirm that all students are progressing toward mastery of key concepts and skills. |
| Developing, adopting, adapting formative assessments that align specifically to the concepts and skills students were expected to learn | The collaborative review of common formative assessment results leads teachers to refine and improve their intervention and enrichment teaching practices so more students are likely to make greater progress toward mastery of the concepts and skills assessed. | Teams regularly engage in reviewing the results of common formative assessments together. A major goal of collaboration is to improve instruction so more students will master the concepts and skills taught. | Teachers use the results of the first common formative assessment to plan how they will improve instruction in ways that enhance learning results. | Teams of teachers do not have common formative assessments that build their capacity to use learning results to enhance teaching and learning. |

(Continued)

Table 6.2 (Continued)

| | Blazing New Paths of Equity/Excellence (Exemplary) | Entering a Whole New Environment (Approaching) | At Early Mile Markers (Developing) | At the Highway On-Ramp (Waiting) |
|---|---|---|---|---|
| Developing and refining daily teaching practices that help monitor, confirm, and enhance the learning of important concepts and skills | The collaborative lesson planning that occurs before teachers begin preparing students for a common formative assessment helps teachers refine and improve their initial teaching practices so more students are likely to make greater progress toward mastery of the concepts and skills assessed. | Before teachers begin preparing students for a common formative assessment, they regularly engage in lesson planning that will help teachers know how to monitor and confirm their students' acquisition of the building blocks that will lead students to master the standard that is the focus of the common formative assessment. | Teacher teams use their first common formative assessment to spur lesson planning that will help teachers know how to monitor and confirm their students' acquisition of the building blocks that will lead students to master the standard that is the focus of the common formative assessment. | Whether or not teachers have common formative assessments, they don't know what to expect their students to know or be able to do as a result of each day's lesson. |

(Continued)

Table 6.2 (Continued)

| | Blazing New Paths of Equity/Excellence (Exemplary) | Entering a Whole New Environment (Approaching) | At Early Mile Markers (Developing) | At the Highway On-Ramp (Waiting) |
|---|---|---|---|---|
| Ensuring that the information acquired from monitoring and confirming learning is communicated effectively to students and family members | By regularly communicating information about common formative assessments to students and parents, educators empower students and parents to advance their mastery of challenging academic concepts and skills. | Teams regularly use their common formative assessments to communicate to students and parents about the important concepts and skills students will be expected to master. As well, when the assessment is administered, teachers communicate to students and parents about what students have learned and what they have not yet learned. | Teacher teams communicate with students and parents about the concepts and skills to be assessed in the first common formative assessment. As well, when the assessment is administered, teachers communicate to students and parents about what students have learned and what they have not yet learned. | In most of the school's classrooms, neither students nor their parents know the extent to which students have mastered important concepts and skills. |

# References

DuFour, R., & Marzano, R. J. (2011). *Leaders of learning: How district, school, and classroom leaders improve student achievement*. Bloomington, IN: Solution Tree.

Fisher, D., & Frey, N. (2007). *Checking for understanding: Formative assessment techniques for your classroom*. Alexandria, VA: ASCD.

Hattie, J. (2023). *Visible learning: The sequel*. New York: Routledge and Taylor & Francis Group.

Johnson, J. F., Uline, C. L., & Perez, L. G. (2019). *Teaching practices from America's Best Urban Schools: A guide for school and classroom leaders*. New York: Routledge and Taylor & Francis Group.

Marzano, R. J. (2003). *What works in schools: Translating research into action*. Alexandria, VA: ASCD.

Senge, P., Cambron-McCabe, N., Lucas, T., Smith, B., Dutton, J., & Kleiner, A. (2012). *Schools that learn: A fifth discipline fieldbook for educators, parents, and everyone who cares about education*. New York: Crown Business.

Stiggins, R. (2017). *The perfect assessment system*. Alexandria, VA: ASCD.

Wiggins, G. P., & McTighe, J. (2005). *Understanding by design: Expanded* (2nd ed.). Alexandria, VA: ASCD.

# 7 | Effective Intervention and Enrichment

> **Voices of Students and Parents From America's Best Schools**
>
> It's like they have a system here. When I met my child's first-grade teacher, I thought, "Oh my gosh, she's a great teacher. I don't think there's a better teacher than her." Then, I met the second-grade teacher and I thought, "She's awesome! A great teacher." Then, when I met the third-grade teacher, I thought, "She's the best!" How do they do that? They've got a system to help make sure all our kids have great teachers.
> — Parent of a Benavides student, Brownsville, TX
>
> One time we had a math assignment and I got two questions wrong, but the next day, I learned how to think about the problems and answer them correctly. Then, I did a similar assignment and I got 100%. I got an "A."
> — Maribel, fourth-grade student at Benavides Elementary, Brownsville, TX
>
> One of the books we're reading is *The Tiger Rising*. I like the book because it's about learning to stand up for one another and help one another. It's a really good book.
> — Leonard, fourth-grade student at LEAD (formerly Concourse Village), South Bronx, NY
>
> For a lot of people in leadership roles, work is just a job and it's not something they're passionate about. Here, Dr. Sorden looks at each

child as if she birthed that child. Okay, I'll be honest, because at first I thought, "Oh, this is going to be a pit stop. It's a public school, and I'm not too keen on the public school system." But when my husband and I saw the way the principal treats the kids here, that was very heavy. We said, "Oh, our son is staying here."

– Parent of a third-grade student at LEAD<br>(formerly Concourse Village), South Bronx, NY

## VIGNETTE M: Benavides Elementary, Brownsville, Texas

### WON NCUST'S AMERICA'S BEST SCHOOL AWARD IN 2015, 2016, 2020, AND 2024

*"It starts with children being respected and knowing they are loved,"* explained Principal Almanza. At Benavides Elementary in Brownsville, Texas, respecting and loving students also means expecting them to excel. For example, teachers make sure all students read and enjoy reading by December of their kindergarten year. Expectations grow at each successive grade level as teachers strive to help students master state standards (not just pass the state assessment). As part of a Black History month celebration, the school librarian posted pictures of many famous Black leaders adjacent to QR codes. At the school's open house, when proud parents scanned QR codes with their phones, they saw videos of their children reading stories about the leaders. Principal Almanza explained, "When we teach, we want our students to truly understand. We want children to understand they are learning about real life. With every standard we teach, we want children to relate to what they're learning."

With over 860 students in prekindergarten through fifth grade (98% of whom identify as Latino/Hispanic and 83% of whom meet low-income criteria), Benavides students outperform the average of all students in Texas at every grade level, in each subject area. This noteworthy accomplishment does not occur by chance. It is pursued intentionally, thoughtfully, and passionately.

Continuously, Benavides educators examine evidence of learning to determine how well students are mastering challenging academic concepts. When data suggest students (one child or many) have not yet achieved high expectations, plans are tailored to ensure academic success. For example, after analyzing students' extended responses to writing prompts, it became clear that some students required additional support. Teacher teams worked together (with support from the bilingual department) to develop plans that lead to improved writing.

In another instance, Principal Almanza shared that Benavides received a new student from China who did not speak English. The principal worked with the team to develop a plan to support the student. The plan included technology to allow the child to hear stories in Chinese that the child could then learn in English. Additionally, the plan included many opportunities for the child to work with classmates who were proficient English speakers.

Success at Benavides starts with students feeling respected and loved. At the same time, however, the many efforts to ensure that all students experience success contribute greatly to students feeling respected and loved.

## VIGNETTE N: P.S. 359, Leaders of Excellence, Advocacy, and Discovery (LEAD), Bronx, New York City, New York (formerly Concourse Village Elementary)

### WON NCUST'S AMERICA'S BEST SCHOOL AWARD IN 2020 AND 2025*

In New York's South Bronx, almost all students at LEAD meet low-income criteria, almost all identify as students of color, and almost all demonstrate proficiency on multiple indicators, including New York's state assessments in literacy and mathematics. Students' progress has spurred greater resolve to continue improving outcomes. Recently, LEAD became an international baccalaureate school focused upon developing the intellectual prowess of each student, building each student's sense of themselves and their connection to others, and empowering students to work collaboratively with others to have a positive impact on their community and the world. As well, the school is adding a new grade level each year, evolving from an elementary school to a school serving pre-kindergarten through eighth grade.

When Alexa Sorden became principal in 2013, she and her team initiated numerous strategies to ensure all students (and their families) felt valued and respected as members of the school community. Meticulously, they established and reinforced a set of core values: Integrity, Perseverance, Optimism, Willingness, Empathy, and Respect (I-POWER). Together, educators built a positive, transformational school culture, helping students see themselves as impressive citizens and scholars who exhibited these core values.

An effective leadership team, built upon a departmentalized structure, has also influenced LEAD's success. Teachers work in vertical teams where they acquire individual and collective expertise in either the humanities or STEM subjects and develop well-articulated plans to ensure all students have a high likelihood of achieving or exceeding rigorous state standards at each grade level. Through the departmentalized structure, teachers also work together to create engaging lessons that help students gain, integrate, and apply important academic skills and then use those skills in ways that prepare students to influence constructive change in their communities or in the world.

At LEAD, teachers continuously monitor, confirm, and enhance learning. Students are much more likely to achieve high rates of proficiency on state assessments when everyday instruction is designed to ensure that students have deep understandings of rigorous concepts and skills. Additionally, however, everyday instruction at LEAD is designed to provide precise and timely intervention. Continuously, as teachers check student understanding, they provide immediate intervention in response to student misconceptions. Timely, focused intervention ensures that student misconceptions are not likely to linger, and students have optimal opportunities to learn rigorous concepts and skills.

While LEAD teachers continuously provide intervention, they also continuously provide enriched learning opportunities. As students benefit from real-world opportunities to apply academic skills in practical ways (e.g., through micro-apprenticeships and community improvement projects), students are more likely to learn academic concepts well. In this way, the need for intervention is diminished.

In 2024, 98% of LEAD students achieved proficiency in mathematics, and 100% achieved proficiency in literacy. Nonetheless, the LEAD team strives for continuous improvement of their practice because they see performance on the state assessment as only one step toward their goal of helping ensure all their students succeed in life.

In NCUST award-winning schools, effective intervention and enrichment build upon the actions associated with the other five gears. Effective intervention and enrichment practices strengthen the positive transformational culture experienced by students as they see themselves developing deep understandings of challenging academic content. Similarly, effective intervention and enrichment practices motivate teachers and students to undertake rigorous curricula when they observe these practices help all students master challenging concepts. Teachers grow ever more eager to support each other in improving initial instruction and in monitoring, confirming, and enhancing student learning as they experience the benefit added by effective intervention and enrichment. In NCUST award-winning schools, intervention and enrichment practices are designed to ensure that students develop deep, accurate, and useful understandings that will enhance their future academic success and success in life.

In schools such as Benavides Elementary (Vignette M) and LEAD (Vignette N), the intervention and enrichment gear helps drive all other gears, maximizing the likelihood that students are not merely acquainted with important academic concepts but understand those concepts well enough to define, describe, and differentiate them; explain how they are intended to work; analyze situations when they don't work well; apply the concepts to real problems in their lives and communities; and evaluate the quality of solutions. So often, lessons in these award-winning schools extend beyond the knowledge and skills required by state assessments. Dr. Sorden, principal of LEAD, explained, "We don't test-prep at all. The word doesn't come up in our building. We ensure that the curriculum is rigorous throughout the entire year, starting in prekindergarten. We emphasize good teaching" (Johnson, Uline, & Munro, 2023, p. 88).

When outstanding intervention and enrichment complement the other five gears, traditional test-prep efforts are unnecessary and, perhaps, counterproductive because students learn more than the right answer. They learn why the answer makes sense, and they become skillful at discerning conditions that influence the extent to which an answer might be the optimal choice. As well, with outstanding intervention and enrichment, students do not practice rote responses beyond the point of boredom. Instead, they practice concepts and skills through real-world applications. Thus, students feel empowered to use their knowledge to solve problems and influence constructive change.

# What Leadership Teams Accomplished to Promote Effective Intervention and Enrichment

Traditionally, many educators think intervention is the appropriate response when students have not learned the required academic concepts and skills. In many schools, intervention, remediation, or Tier II instruction is provided subsequent to initial instruction, specifically for students who did not adequately benefit from initial instruction. This instruction often takes place in separate settings, away from students who appear to not need intervention.

Often traditional intervention is less effective than the initial instruction it is intended to remedy because (1) frequently, intervention does not focus upon students' specific misconceptions; (2) intervention often utilizes the same unsuccessful instructional approaches utilized in initial instruction; (3) intervention is often delayed until students have had many opportunities to practice misconceptions until thinking errors are resistant to correction; (4) intervention frequently includes stigmatization because the only students receiving intervention are those perceived to have less academic or intellectual promise; and (5) in some schools, intervention is provided by educators who have less knowledge related to the content or the pedagogical approaches that might help students learn the content, while individuals with greater knowledge and skill are asked to teach students who do not require intervention.

Likewise, enrichment was traditionally perceived as an instructional strategy implemented exclusively for students who demonstrated some measure of proficiency with the concepts and skills presented during initial instruction. While some enrichment lessons provide students rich opportunities to apply important concepts and skills in interesting, engaging situations, in many schools, enrichment is not effective because (1) enrichment activities tend to focus upon busy work that requires students to practice the concepts and skills they have already learned; (2) some enrichment lessons offer students little guidance or support in transitioning from rote procedures to applied thinking; and (3) many educators assume that enrichment is supplemental and nonessential, so there is generally no urgency to ensure that students learn how to apply concepts and skills within real-life situations.

Even when schools provide students excellent academic enrichment, they may systematically exclude students who need intervention from opportunities to benefit from enrichment (because intervention and enrichment opportunities are, too often, offered separately and simultaneously). Students who regularly need intervention tend to fall further and further behind students who regularly receive strong enrichment services.

In *Teaching Practices from America's Best Urban Schools* (Johnson, Uline, & Perez, 2019), the authors discussed intervention and enrichment as part of the coherent education improvement system found in NCUST award-winning schools. In most NCUST award-winning schools, educators found ways to minimize the dysfunctions of traditional intervention and enrichment while maximizing efforts to ensure strong learning results for all students. For example, intervention was tailored to the specific academic needs of students. Frequently, educators provided intervention to individual students or small groups of students intended to address specific misconceptions that interfered with students developing a clear and accurate understanding of a concept.

In some cases, schools provided intervention at times that did not interfere with opportunities to participate in regular classroom programs. For example, several NCUST award-winning middle schools and high schools offered students opportunities to participate in Saturday classes, afterschool tutorials, or intersessions so they could receive additional support while continuing to benefit from the instruction provided in regular classroom programs (Johnson, Uline, & Perez, 2017: Theokas, Gonzáles, Manriquez, & Johnson, 2019). In some schools, educators used a strategy they called "front loading" to introduce concepts and skills early to students who had experienced academic difficulty previously. "Intervention" became prevention as students with additional needs became acquainted with concepts, vocabulary, and skills before their classmates (Johnson et al., 2019).

Similarly, in NCUST award-winning schools, often teachers provided enriching lessons for all students as part of initial instruction. The lessons provided students opportunities to apply concepts and skills to real problems that influenced their lives. Often, teachers provided enriching lessons for all students as part of initial instruction. For example, as Patrick Henry's fifth-grade students (Vignette I) learned challenging state literacy standards, they read Margot Shetterly's *Hidden Figures,* based upon a true story that was popularized by a major motion picture. Students found it easier to analyze text structures, cite textual evidence, or understand variations in characters' viewpoints when they were applying those skills to a text they perceived as engaging, interesting, and relevant to their lives (Johnson et al., 2023).

In recent NCUST award-winning schools, we find evidence of practices that further maximize the benefits, and minimize the dysfunctions, associated with traditional intervention and enrichment. For example, in schools such as Patrick Henry Preparatory School (Vignette I), Silver Wing Elementary (Vignette J), Feaster Charter School (Vignette K), R. F. Hazard Elementary (Vignette L), Benavides Elementary (Vignette M), and LEAD (Vignette N), all students benefit from effective intervention as soon as they need it. As well, all students benefit from academic enrichment that helps them develop deep, practical understandings of important concepts and skills. The provision of intervention and enrichment (not intervention *or* enrichment) becomes a logical way to ensure that all students benefit from a positive, transformational culture and are likely to learn rigorous curricula. In NCUST award-winning schools, this happens as a result of effective initial instruction, punctuated with deliberate efforts to monitor, confirm, and enhance learning.

Through continuous dialogue and persistent checking for understanding, teachers mine their students' thinking and bring to light important misconceptions. In this way, teachers help students refine their own thinking, teaching them how to prevent misconceptions from clouding their understanding. As well, by providing all students rich opportunities to apply concepts and skills to important real-life situations, teachers multiply the likelihood that students will distinguish reasonable possibilities from absurd conclusions. Students will not only learn to identify solutions but will also comprehend the factors that influenced the solutions. They will come to see themselves as problem solvers, change agents, and empowered individuals who can make a difference in their lives and in the world.

To establish effective intervention and enrichment, leadership teams guided their colleagues to accomplish several important shifts in instructional planning and practice. First, leadership teams promoted timely opportunities for all students to benefit from intervention and enrichment that emphasized real-world applications of rigorous concepts/skills. As well, leadership teams promoted intervention and enrichment strategies that were laser focused on the important concepts and skills students needed to master. In particular, leadership teams ensured that educators knew how to observe student thinking and adapt instructional practices accordingly. Finally, leadership teams ensured that teacher teams collaboratively designed intervention and enrichment strategies they perceived as workable and likely to yield outstanding learning results. These strategies were then assessed and improved over time in light of students' ongoing progress.

## Leadership Teams Promoted Timely Opportunities for All Students to Benefit From Intervention and Enrichment That Emphasized Real-World Applications of Rigorous Concepts/Skills

For several years at both Benavides Elementary (Vignette M) and LEAD (Vignette N), leaders emphasized the importance of timely attention to student understanding. In NCUST award-winning schools, teachers don't wait for students to fail to determine how to help students excel (Johnson et al., 2019). Instead, educators are continuously interacting with students. Teachers endeavor to determine, "How is he thinking about this? Does she really understand why this makes sense? Does he know why his answer is correct? What thinking led her to that interesting conclusion?" Teachers behave as if they need to understand how students are thinking *now*, because teachers recognize the complexity of the tasks they are asking their students to perform (Hattie, 2023). They recognize the importance of correcting misconceptions promptly, before they take root, demoralize students, and lead them to conclude, for example, they aren't smart enough to identify the author's intent or to determine how a linear equation could predict the impact of an extra 90 minutes of work and a bonus on their paycheck.

Leadership teams at NCUST award-winning schools worked to ensure that all students developed deep understandings of important concepts and skills in ways that can be applied to real-world challenges and opportunities. In these schools, application to real-world situations is not a luxury reserved for select students. Instead, teachers see real-world application as a tool for helping all their students develop deep understanding of important concepts. At NCUST award-winning schools, educators realize that struggling students may benefit the most from opportunities to see how the concepts and skills they are learning relate to the real world, and specifically to their own lives. At Patrick Henry Preparatory School (Vignette

I), Silver Wing Elementary (Vignette J), Feaster Charter School (Vignette K), R. F. Hazard Elementary (Vignette L), Benavides Elementary (Vignette M), the LEAD School (Vignette N), and many other NCUST award-winning schools, all students benefit from opportunities to learn rigorous literacy standards by reading engaging novels that students consider relevant to their lives. Similarly, at these schools, students learn challenging mathematics and science concepts by working on practical problems that are relevant to their lives, their communities, and their world.

## *Leadership Teams Promoted Intervention and Enrichment Laser Focused on the Important Concepts and Skills Students Needed to Master*

In many NCUST award-winning schools, intervention and enrichment are neither generic nor aimless. Often, prior to providing instruction, leadership teams support their colleagues in pre-identifying critical concepts and skills associated with each academic standard they endeavor to teach. Then, leadership teams support educators in developing questioning strategies or other learning tasks to determine if students understand the relevant concepts and skills appropriately. For example, as teachers listen to students in collaborative conversations, as they read the explanations students write on their whiteboards, as they observe student groups plan steps for initiating a project, and as they review students' entries into software to explain the thinking behind their choice of an algorithm, teachers identify the specific concepts, skills, thinking patterns, big ideas, small nuances, *and* misunderstandings that will become the focus of immediate instructional attention.

At some struggling schools, we have observed teachers who ask students to engage in discussions about concepts; however, teachers seem to miss hearing the errors in students' responses. We have seen teachers ask students to write responses on individual whiteboards; however, teachers seem to not notice that some students write incorrect responses. As well, we have seen some teachers ask students to write descriptions that show how they arrived at a specific answer; however, teachers seem not to notice that, even though a student acquired the correct answer, the student used a strategy that will not lead to accurate answers in most situations. In all these cases, teachers seem to understand the value of students' engagement in demonstrating their understanding; however, the teachers may not fully grasp the value of their efforts to understand how their students think.

At NCUST award-winning schools, leadership teams helped their colleagues see the value of probing to understand what students thought or how students thought about concepts, strategies, or skills. When teachers better understood their students' thinking, they were better prepared to plan effective intervention that would correct misconceptions. As well, teachers could better plan effective enrichment that would deepen understanding and application of newly learned concepts and skills. In NCUST award-winning schools, leadership teams helped their colleagues learn how to observe student thinking and then make wise instructional decisions that promoted deep understanding. For example, a parent at LEAD (Vignette N) explained, "The teachers here know my child. They know how he thinks. So, they make sure he's going to learn and succeed."

With a clear understanding of the critical concepts, skills, or strategies students will need to utilize and with up-to-the-minute information about students' understanding and use of these critical concepts, skills, or strategies, educators are prepared to provide laser-focused intervention and enrichment. Intervention and enrichment can be tailored just in time and right on point to help students see what they need to see or experience to develop a deeper, more accurate understanding of the important concepts, skills, and strategies that will lead them to master rigorous academic standards.

This does not mean that teachers in NCUST award-winning schools are constantly providing students correct answers. In contrast, teachers know their students well enough to determine how much struggle will be productive in helping students develop deep academic understandings. Teachers structure intervention and enrichment experiences that will provide students sufficient challenge to maximize meaningful learning while also providing sufficient support to ensure students are likely to succeed with appropriate effort. As a result of the laser focus on the specific concepts and skills students need to master, students waste little time feeling stuck and confused. In contrast, students perceive they are continuously learning, growing, and developing levels of proficiency that will help them succeed in school and in life.

## *Leadership Teams Ensured Teacher Teams Collaboratively Designed Intervention and Enrichment Strategies They Perceived as Workable and Likely to Yield Outstanding Learning Results*

In many NCUST award-winning schools, teacher collaboration meetings became the drawing rooms for crafting effective intervention and enrichment plans. For instance, at Feaster Charter School (Vignette K), the sixth-grade team met to review student work products. While they recognized many of their students benefited from initial instruction and could read a complex passage and cite textual evidence to support their analysis of the text, they also recognized many of their students had not yet demonstrated mastery of the objective. The team did not simply put grades in a gradebook and move on to the next objective. As well, teachers did not simply plan intervention that repeated the initial instruction they provided. Instead, they looked thoughtfully at their students' work, and they thought about how instruction could be refined to address possible student misconceptions. They listened as some teachers talked about the strategies that had been most helpful to their students, and they made plans to adopt or adapt those strategies to help other students. Their collaborative planning resulted in teachers developing plans of action that were more likely to correct misconceptions and were also more likely to help students strengthen their application of appropriate strategies.

In NCUST award-winning schools, intervention and enrichment are tailored to build upon what students have demonstrated they know, correct students' specific misconceptions, and develop the thinking processes that will serve students well as they approach similar problems throughout their lives. Effective intervention and enrichment help ensure all students perceive themselves as bright, capable scholars with infinite capacity to learn challenging academic skills. At the same time, effective intervention and enrichment help ensure educators develop a sense of collective efficacy that helps them see themselves as a powerful team of professionals with outstanding capacity to educate every student group well.

## Why Promoting Effective Intervention and Enrichment Is Challenging Yet Rewarding

To promote effective intervention and enrichment, leadership teams must disrupt old, often counter-productive practices and routines. Even when teachers recognize that their intervention and enrichment routines are ineffective, change is difficult because patterns have been ingrained into the fabric of many schools.

The first problematic, ingrained pattern is the either/or paradigm that suggests some students need intervention because they have not adequately learned critical concepts or skills and other students have earned enrichment because they have demonstrated mastery of the critical concepts and skills. In contrast, NCUST award-winning schools demonstrate that all students can benefit from timely, laser-focused, collaboratively designed intervention and enrichment. The second problematic, ingrained pattern is the notion that both intervention and enrichment occur subsequent to initial instruction. In contrast, in NCUST award-winning schools we find both intervention and enrichment occurring as educators engage in initial instruction.

These patterns may be difficult to change; however, as described in Table 7.1, the success of NCUST award-winning schools suggest that change efforts can be worthwhile. By providing all students timely access to effective intervention and enrichment, schools can lead many more students to high levels of academic success, as measured by state assessments, success in advanced classes, and many other indicators.

Table 7.1 Challenges and Rewards of Effective Intervention and Enrichment

| Issue | The Challenges | The Rewards |
| --- | --- | --- |
| **Promoting timely opportunities for all students to benefit from intervention and enrichment that emphasizes real-world applications of rigorous concepts/skills** | To ensure all students benefit from timely intervention, leadership teams should help educators develop systems for checking student understanding during initial instruction and adapting learning activities accordingly. To ensure all students benefit from enriching real-world applications of concepts/skills, leadership teams should help educators integrate applied activities into initial instruction. Both may require sustained professional development. | When all students experience access to timely intervention and enriching lessons that apply the concepts learned to real-life situations, all students will have greater opportunities to achieve mastery of concepts and experience success in school and in life. |
| **Promoting intervention and enrichment that are laser focused on the important concepts and skills students need to master** | To ensure teachers provide intervention and enrichment that are laser focused on the important concepts and skills students need to master, teachers need support with (1) identifying critical concepts and skills associated with each standard, (2) using questioning strategies or other tasks to determine if students have learned those concepts and skills well, and (3) designing intervention and enrichment approaches that will help their students master the critical concepts and skills. | When leadership teams support educators in learning how to design intervention and enrichment experiences that are laser focused on the concepts and skills students need to master, all students are more likely to experience high levels of academic success. |

(Continued)

Table 7.1 (Continued)

| Issue | The Challenges | The Rewards |
|---|---|---|
| **Ensuring teacher teams collaboratively designed intervention and enrichment strategies they perceive as workable and likely to yield outstanding learning results** | To ensure that intervention and enrichment are designed collaboratively in ways that work for teachers and in ways that maximize student learning, collaboration time must be set aside, it must be structured in a way that teachers perceive as supportive, and it must be led by individuals who are skillful in helping teachers consider what students understand and what they have not yet understood. Collaboration time must result in teachers being prepared to provide timely, laser-focused intervention and enrichment. | When teachers perceive they have abundant support from their colleagues in developing effective intervention and enrichment, teachers are much more likely to share a sense of collective efficacy and believe that, as a team, they will lead all their students to high levels of success in school and in life. |

# Effective Intervention and Enrichment: What It Is and What It Isn't

**(X) What It Isn't: Intervention for Some Students and Enrichment for Others**

In many schools, some students receive intervention assistance when other students receive enrichment. Often this approach widens the opportunity-to-learn gap experienced by some students. Many students receiving intervention get a second dose of the instructional strategies that were ineffective during initial instruction, while other students benefit from opportunities to learn how the concepts and skills they are studying can be applied to relevant situations.

**(✓) What It Is: Intervention and Enrichment for All**

In NCUST award-winning schools, it is common to find all students benefitting from timely, laser-focused intervention, as well as relevant and practical enrichment opportunities that allow students to apply concepts and skills to familiar situations. All students benefit from instruction that is responsive to their individual understandings and their individual needs for deeper understandings. Simultaneously, all students benefit from instruction that provides students opportunities to learn how they can use the academic concepts and skills they are learning to address real issues in their lives, their communities, and their world.

**(X) What It Isn't: Intervention That Happens Only After the Unit Is Completed**

In many schools, intervention occurs only after the unit is completed, the assessment is given and scored, and students are identified who did not master the concept and skills they were expected to learn. Often, however, the misconceptions that led students not to master the concept began developing long before the assessment was administered. In many cases, students have multiple opportunities to "practice" misconceptions before intervention is initiated. One veteran educational leader discussed this phenomenon by noting, "Practice may or may not make perfect, but it certainly goes far to make permanent."

## ✓ What It Is: Intervention That Is Integrated Into Initial Instruction

In NCUST award-winning schools, teachers continuously check to determine what and how students understand important concepts and skills. When teachers recognize misconceptions in student thinking, they intervene immediately with strategies to help students see their thinking errors, understand why the error occurred, and develop strategies for reducing the likelihood the error will occur in the future.

## ✗ What It Isn't: Intervention That Is Generic

In some schools, intervention activities are the same for all students who need additional assistance. As a result, some students do not benefit when the intervention activities don't address their specific academic needs.

## ✓ What It Is: Intervention and Enrichment That Are Laser Focused

In NCUST award-winning schools, neither intervention nor enrichment is generic. Typically, intervention is designed in response to a specific academic concern presented by one student or a group of students. As a result, intervention frequently helps students correct their misconceptions and develop solid understandings. As well, enrichment is often targeted in ways that offer students opportunities to apply specific concepts and skills they are learning to real situations that influence their lives.

## ✗ What It Isn't: Intervention and Enrichment Designed by Teachers Working Independently

In many schools, educators develop intervention and enrichment lessons independently. They have limited opportunity to benefit from their colleagues' perspectives and skills related to pinpointing issues that influence their students' misunderstandings about important concepts and skills. Similarly, teachers who develop intervention and enrichment lessons without the support of colleagues have limited opportunity to learn from their colleagues ideas about how to design engaging lessons that help students apply the concepts they are learning to solve real problems influencing students' lives or their communities. As a result, in typical schools, intervention and enrichment are often very similar to the initial instruction teachers provide.

## ✓ What It Is: Intervention and Enrichment Designed Collaboratively by Teams of Teachers

In NCUST award-winning schools, educators spend considerable time supporting each other in collaboratively designing intervention and enrichment. Teachers work together to identify important issues that may pose stumbling blocks to student understanding. Often, one educator's insights into her students' misconceptions help explain the student errors other teachers identify. In award-winning schools, teachers pool their insights in ways that help their colleagues develop interesting, precise, and effective lessons that lead all students to deeper understandings of important concepts and skills.

# Tips for Leadership Teams

*How Schools Can Promote Effective Intervention and Enrichment (Remember to Review and Implement These Tips Regularly)*

- If your school has not yet set aside time for teams of teachers to work together to plan intervention and enrichment lessons, the leadership team should carefully consider options for doing so. Setting aside even a few minutes per week can open the door for extended teacher collaboration.

- If time has been set aside for teacher collaboration concerning intervention and enrichment lessons, the leadership team should consider developing meeting agenda formats that could help teacher teams more effectively address intervention and enrichment issues. For example, leadership teams could provide agendas that encourage their colleagues to pre-identify the critical concepts and skills associated with each academic standard that could be a potential stumbling block. Planning agendas could then encourage educators to support each other in developing questioning strategies and/or other tasks to determine if students understand those concepts and skills appropriately. Additionally, planning agendas could encourage teacher teams to identify strategies for reducing the likelihood of specific misconceptions or helping students correct their misconceptions when they emerge. As well, planning agendas could encourage teacher teams to identify highly engaging and enriching lesson activities that allow students to apply the concepts and skills they are learning to real-life problems.

- Through teacher collaboration meetings, professional learning activities, and/or peer observations, the leadership team should support teachers in investigating the reasons behind student misunderstandings of academic concepts and skills. As teachers increase their skill at identifying the source of students' misconceptions, they will increase their ability to prevent misconceptions and to guide students in correcting misconceptions.

- The leadership team should consider how professional learning activities could encourage teachers to refine their best enrichment lessons so they could be part of the initial instruction provided to all students. The leadership team should consider ideas for allowing teachers to observe such lessons and then try to implement similar lessons with affirming, supportive feedback from peers.

# Where Is Your School on the Road to Promoting Effective Intervention and Enrichment?

The school leadership team should consider using the rubric in Table 7.2 to assess the school's progress toward promoting effective intervention and enrichment. By reviewing the rubric each semester, the leadership team may identify and celebrate areas of growth and identify areas where additional growth is needed.

Table 7.2 Rubric for Assessing the School's Progress Promoting Effective Intervention and Enrichment

| | Blazing New Paths of Equity/Excellence (Exemplary) | Entering a Whole New Environment (Approaching) | At Early Mile Markers (Developing) | At the Highway On-Ramp (Waiting) |
|---|---|---|---|---|
| **Promoting timely opportunities for all students to benefit from intervention and enrichment that emphasizes real-world applications of rigorous concepts/skills** | Over time, teachers develop expertise as they help each other implement timely intervention and enrichment practices. Increasingly, student misunderstandings are addressed promptly in ways that result in higher levels of mastery. | Throughout the school, teacher teams support each other in developing and refining practices that support timely intervention and enrichment. | The leadership team organizes professional learning activities that help teachers learn how to identify student misconceptions early and respond immediately with effective intervention and enrichment. | Generally, teachers provide intervention to students long after misconceptions start developing. Students rarely receive lessons that allow them to use the concepts they learn to solve real problems. |
| **Promoting intervention and enrichment that are laser focused on the important concepts and skills students need to master** | Over time, teachers develop expertise as they help each other identify specific misconceptions and design focused and effective intervention and enrichment practices. Increasingly, students demonstrate high levels of understanding. | Throughout the school, teacher teams support each other in developing and refining practices that support highly focused intervention and enrichment activities that enhance student understanding. | The leadership team organizes professional learning activities that help teachers learn how to focus both intervention and enrichment activities in ways that are likely to rectify student misconceptions. | Generally, teachers do not know the misconceptions that might interfere with student understanding, so intervention and enrichment tend to be generic. |

(Continued)

Table 7.2 (Continued)

| | Blazing New Paths of Equity/Excellence (Exemplary) | Entering a Whole New Environment (Approaching) | At Early Mile Markers (Developing) | At the Highway On-Ramp (Waiting) |
|---|---|---|---|---|
| Ensuring that intervention and enrichment are collaboratively designed by teacher teams in ways teachers perceive workable and likely to yield outstanding learning results | The planning and implementation of intervention and enrichment lessons improves consistently as teachers benefit from effective collaboration. Students experience increasingly high levels of mastery because of the quality of instruction that results from teacher collaboration. | Most teachers plan intervention and enrichment lessons with the support of colleagues. Teachers support each other in learning best practices for helping students develop deep understandings of concepts and skills. | The leadership team ensures that every teacher will benefit from opportunities to engage in some regular, useful cooperative planning of intervention and enrichment lessons. | Generally, teachers plan and design intervention and enrichment lessons individually without support from their colleagues. |

# References

Hattie, J. (2023). *Visible learning: The sequel.* New York: Routledge and Taylor & Francis Group.

Johnson, J. F., Uline, C. L., & Munro, S. J. (2023). *When Black students excel: How schools can engage and empower Black students.* New York: Routledge and Taylor & Francis Group.

Johnson, J. F., Uline, C. L., & Perez, L. G. (2017). *Leadership in America's best urban schools.* New York: Routledge and Taylor & Francis Group.

Johnson, J. F., Uline, C. L., & Perez, L. G. (2019). *Teaching practices from America's Best Urban Schools: A guide for school and classroom leaders.* New York: Routledge and Taylor & Francis Group.

Theokas, C., Gonzáles, M. L., Manriquez, C., & Johnson, J. F. (2019). *Five practices for improving the success of Latino students: A guide for secondary school leaders.* New York: Routledge and Taylor & Francis Group.

# 8 The Role of District Leaders

### VIGNETTE O: Brownsville Independent School District Brownsville, Texas

*Brownsville Independent School District is perched at the southern tip of Texas, immediately north of the Rio Grande and Matamoros, Mexico. Almost all of the district's 36,000 students identify as Latino or Hispanic (98%), almost all come from families that meet low-income criteria (89%), and many are emerging as multi-lingual learners (30%). All seven of the high schools are "Early College High Schools" offering students opportunities to earn college credit while they pursue high school diplomas. The U.S. Department of Education has recognized six of the district's elementary schools and one of the high schools as National Blue Ribbon Schools. As well, three of the high schools, one middle school, and nine elementary schools are NCUST award-winning schools. Brownsville ISD has more NCUST award-winning schools than any district in the nation.*

*For many years, Brownsville district leaders have deliberately, persistently, and passionately pursued academic success for all the district's students. District leaders have supported principals and their leadership teams in ways that have influenced impressive improvements in learning outcomes for students. The district superintendent explained that an important part of his job was to keep the school board focused on the important work of improving schools. He recognized that the district played a key role in helping schools move the gears that drive student learning. He told the board, "If you want this district to continue to improve, then you've got to make the investment. . . . Our investment is our staff development program."* Brownsville ISD hires strong school and classroom leaders and then supports those leaders in working together to create life-changing opportunities for students.

One of the district's curriculum and instruction executive directors added, *"Our schools are an example of an effective school framework. . . . Each school has high-quality instruction, a culture of students first, and a very strong culture of keeping everyone involved (parents, community, and the teachers). Staff members take pride in what they do. So, it starts with strong leadership, but at the core, we keep the students in mind. As a district, we continue that model of effective schools and continue improving."*

---

In Chapters 1 through 7, we described how school leadership teams can influence substantially greater learning outcomes for all demographic groups of students. In this chapter, we focus on how district leaders can support or guide school leadership teams in ways that build their capacity to influence positive learning outcomes for all student groups.

Whenever NCUST teams visit finalists for the America's Best Schools Award, the teams interview district leaders (often superintendents and the individuals who directly supervise principals) to learn more about the district's role in the finalist's success. Often, we find outstanding district leaders who relentlessly pursue academic excellence for all students in their districts. This chapter shares our preliminary findings regarding district leadership practices that supported the establishment and implementation of outstanding school leadership teams who drove the success of all student groups.

Rorrer, Skrla, and Scheurich (2008) explained that districts play a pivotal role in educational reform. Their synthesis of research on the district's role in reform identified four key functions of districts: providing instructional leadership, reorienting the organization, establishing policy coherence, and maintaining an equity focus. To achieve sustainable reform, district leaders must establish structures that support site leaders effectively. The superintendent, as lead architect of district coherence, plays a critical role in aligning the district's structures and vision. In our research, we have found that NCUST award-winning schools' successes have been positively influenced by district leaders who provide instructional leadership, reorient the district in ways that focus energy and resources on critical needs and opportunities, establish coherent policy that supports academic excellence for all students, and maintain a persistent focus on improving learning outcomes for every student group.

The superintendent's role has grown in complexity over the last few decades. Once perceived primarily as a CEO who managed board relations and policy alignment, the superintendent now resembles an orchestra conductor, harmonizing diverse stakeholder actions while mitigating discord from various interest groups. Superintendents must ensure that six interlocking gears – effective leadership teams; positive transformational culture; rigorous curricula; monitoring, confirming, and enhancing learning; effective initial instruction; and intervention and enrichment – function cohesively to drive student success. Moreover, they must navigate political landscapes to prevent misalignment that could stall instructional progress. Building a central office leadership team impervious to political pressures and committed to supporting these essential elements at every school site has become a key superintendent function.

## What District Leaders Do to Help Schools Improve Learning Outcomes for All Students

We propose four strategies district leaders can utilize to help their schools accelerate movement of the six gears and generate greater learning outcomes for all students. The first two strategies are part of the district coherence framework articulated by Fullan and Quinn (2016). The district coherence framework emphasizes focusing direction, cultivating collaborative cultures, deepening learning, and securing accountability. The first two strategies (focusing direction and cultivating collaborative cultures) are particularly relevant to the role district leaders play in helping schools advance the six gears that drive improved learning outcomes for all students. It is noteworthy that Fullan and Quinn's district coherence framework was influenced by the successes of the Garden Grove Unified School District in Southern California, home of six NCUST award-winning schools.

## *District Leaders Focus Direction in Ways That Emphasize the Overarching Purpose of Improvement Efforts*

In the Garden Grove Unified School District, the Brownsville Independent School District (Vignette O), and in several other districts that have developed and supported NCUST award-winning schools (e.g., the Chula Vista Elementary School District in Southern California, the Miami-Dade County School District in Florida, and the Fort Worth Independent School District in Texas), district leaders have focused direction by emphasizing the moral imperative of improving learning outcomes in ways that will positively influence all students' lives. These district leaders do more than deliver eloquent speeches about improving schools for the benefit of children. They describe clear, logical strategies for supporting district-wide change that will lead to specific, measurable improvements. For example, Brownsville's Superintendent Chavez helped his school board understand why and how the district would invest effort in building the capacity of the district's staff (See Vignette O). Similarly, Knudson (2013) described how both the previous and the current superintendent in Garden Grove defined the "Garden Grove Way" as practical, district-wide strategies for improving school culture, curriculum, and instruction. Generally, district leaders first emphasize the changes in district-level structures and actions that will be necessary to better support schools. Then, leaders emphasize how school personnel can utilize the district's support to make important improvements in teaching and learning that will accelerate student success. Johnson, Uline, and Perez (2017) emphasized that successful leaders articulate clear reasons for pursuing change in ways that resonate with stakeholders and highlight the impact on students. Instead of doggedly insisting upon compliance, successful district leaders inspire commitment, as stakeholders observe evidence of their leaders' determination to achieve what stakeholders yearn to achieve. Perhaps most importantly, district leaders stay focused on the direction they articulate. They don't allow the district to become distracted with the fads of the year or consumed by the political issues of the day. Stakeholders see the district's stability as a sign of the organization's reliability, sincerity, and commitment.

## *District Leaders Model, Nurture, and Support the Development of Collaborative Cultures*

Fullan and Quinn's district coherence framework also emphasizes the importance of cultivating collaborative cultures. Specifically, they wrote:

> Charismatic heroes will not save the day. Rather, we need leaders who create a culture of growth; know how to engage the hearts and minds of everyone; and focus their collective intelligence, talent, and commitment to shaping a new path. They recognize that what pulls people in is meaningful work in collaboration with others. They *use the group to change the group* by building deep collaborative work horizontally and vertically across their organizations.
> 
> (Fullan & Quinn, 2016, p. 47)

Many NCUST award-winning schools have benefitted from district leaders who have helped school leaders cultivate collaboration as fuel for school-wide improvement. Unfortunately, most U.S. schools are not structured to support meaningful collaboration. Where meaningful collaboration occurs, district leaders have worked with teachers, administrators, and policy makers to create a specific time frame for collaboration. Just as importantly, district leaders have built and sustained cultures that facilitate productive, collaborative interactions. Effective leaders understand that meaningful collaboration requires trust. If educators, administrators, and other stakeholders do not perceive their opportunities to collaborate are consistently grounded in a culture that is honest, open, trustworthy, well intentioned, and competent, collaboration is likely to be shallow, compliance driven, and minimally impactful (Tschannen-Moran, 2014). Trust also requires stability. Districts with revolving doors on the superintendent's office have greater challenges developing and maintaining the level of trust needed to engage the sustained commitment of stakeholders. Similarly, superintendents who put revolving doors on principal's offices often create a culture that diminishes the commitment of school personnel, family, and students as principals come and go before meaningful trust is established.

Without successful collaboration, none of the six gears described in this book are likely to move. Collaboration is the fundamental work of effective school leadership teams. The creation of positive transformational cultures for school personnel, and for all demographic groups of students, requires extensive collaboration among school personnel, students, and families. Efforts to establish rigorous curricula school-wide hinge on the quality of horizontal and vertical collaboration throughout a school. The ongoing improvement of initial instruction; the monitoring, confirming, and enhancing of learning; and the continuous improvement of intervention and enrichment depend upon the extent to which schools create and sustain collaborative structures in which educators are eager to learn from each other, and with each other, as they continuously improve their craft. District leaders facilitate successful collaboration by helping stakeholders know their knowledge, insight, commitment, and skill are essential to school-wide and district-wide efforts to improve learning outcomes for all student groups.

As well, district leaders support a culture of collaboration by selecting and developing leaders (including central office leaders, principals, and teacher leaders) who believe in the power of collaboration and know how to cultivate and sustain effective collaboration. If stakeholders do not perceive leaders value their ideas, experience, and perspectives, or do not appreciate their commitment and effort, they will not invest effort in regular and sustained collaboration. In districts such as Brownsville ISD and Garden Grove USD, superintendents recognized the importance of ensuring that leaders at all levels know how to support and sustain effective collaboration.

## *District Leaders Support Change by Helping Schools Measure the Movement of the Six Gears*

A third area of district-level influence and support addresses school leadership teams' confidence and expertise in measuring the changes they endeavor to pursue. Bryk, Gomez, Grunow, and LeMahieu (2015) distinguished measurement for improvement from measurement for accountability. Often, districts focus exclusively on measurement for accountability such as end-of-year assessment results and teacher evaluation results. Conversely, districts often have very few measures to gauge improvement in the processes they believe will influence better learning results.

District leaders can support school leadership teams by helping schools develop and appropriately utilize practical measures to determine the quantity and quality of movement of each of the six gears. Practical measures may include a variety of qualitative and quantitative tools for determining the extent to which, and how well, a desired process is occurring. For example, a practical measure to determine if students from all racial/ethnic groups feel welcome, respected, and valued at school may be a series of empathy interviews sampling students from each racial/ethnic group. A practical measure to determine how teachers check students' depth of understanding may be a classroom observation protocol that allows an observer to record the various strategies teachers use to learn what, and how well, students understand. Such practical measures seek to support improvement, not to cast blame. Therefore, when measures indicate intended improvement has not occurred, wise leaders do not assume individuals are incompetent or insubordinate (Johnson et al., 2017). Rather, wise leaders first ask the question, "How does the system need to improve to help individuals successfully improve implementation?"

Without ongoing measurement of improvement, educators might assume they have successfully implemented a change when, in fact, nothing significant has changed. Educators who join their colleagues in reading this book might assume they already effectively move the six gears that drive improved learning outcomes. In the absence of progress measures, deep understanding of the six gears, and their purpose, will remain elusive. As well, in the absence of measurement of accountability, leadership teams can easily pursue processes that make little difference to students' academic success. When efforts link evidence of improvements in critical processes with evidence of improvement in important educational outcomes, systems can accelerate learning for students, as the system accelerates its own learning.

## *District Leaders Nurture a Culture of Continuous Improvement*

Finally, district leaders can help school leadership teams improve student-learning outcomes by nurturing a culture that supports continuous improvement processes. The work of improving teaching and learning is never done (Chenoweth, 2021). In the highest-performing, most celebrated schools, we frequently hear educators acknowledge their need to continue learning how to better support their students. As one NCUST award-winning leader shared, "We did great with last year's students, but this year we have a new group with different needs and different abilities. We have to keep getting better!"

District leaders can support improvement processes, first, by encouraging appreciative inquiry about schools that achieve remarkable results for all students. Chenoweth argued, "Success and improvement hold lessons for anyone willing to look at the data and say: 'Your students are doing better than mine. What are you doing?'" (2021, p. 142). Many leaders of NCUST award-winning schools have claimed their journey to success included visits to and/or conversations with leaders from other high-performing schools. District leaders can support ongoing improvement processes by providing opportunities for school leadership teams to observe and learn from the improvement processes implemented at schools that achieve remarkable learning outcomes for similar students.

At the same time, wise district leaders know the importance of identifying, acknowledging, and celebrating evidence of growth within schools that are struggling to improve learning outcomes. It takes time for schools to generate outstanding outcomes for all students. Unfortunately, some district leaders impatiently insist upon immediate excellent results. In doing so, they might ignore the promising efforts of principals and leadership teams to initiate coherent and consistent movement of the six gears, positioning their schools so improved outcomes are likely to follow. Even worse, district leaders' insistence upon immediate excellent results may push principals and leadership teams to ignore the six gears and focus upon superficial strategies that yield an immediate bump in accountability results that is not likely to be sustained.

To advance a district-wide culture of continuous improvement, district leaders must skillfully define principles the district will hold "tightly" and practices the district will hold "loosely," affording school leaders appropriate flexibility to build upon their school's strengths and respond to their specific needs. For example, in some districts with multiple NCUST award-winning schools, we find leaders who tightly insist that each school develop comprehensive efforts to improve learning outcomes for students who historically have not been served well. District leaders may insist that school plans include attention to key elements that have proven powerful in improving learning outcomes (e.g., the six gears). However, the district leaders may allow school leadership teams flexibility to tailor their comprehensive efforts in response to the strengths and needs of their students and their school personnel. Schools that demonstrate progress toward improved outcomes for the specific student groups are rewarded with continued flexibility; however, schools that do not demonstrate progress receive support, guidance, and, ultimately, less flexibility. WestEd (2019) reported how the "tight-loose strategy" had positively influenced outcomes in the Chula Vista Elementary School District (CVESD) near San Diego, California. CVESD is the home of eight NCUST award-winning schools.

In some school districts, every district initiative is "tight" with a series of mandates that offer school leadership teams little flexibility to adjust practices in response to their strengths and needs. In contrast, in some school districts, everything is perennially "loose," promoting a laissez-faire culture in which mediocre approaches may be sustained for decades. The most successful districts develop and sustain a culture of continuous improvement by focusing direction with clear expectations for strong learning outcomes for all groups of students; building, nurturing, and sustaining collaborative structures that support educators and leaders as everyone learns to improve their efforts, measuring improvements in implementation as well as improvements in outcomes; and acknowledging and celebrating improvements in learning outcomes, as well as improvements in processes that are likely to lead to improved learning outcomes.

## Why District Leadership Support Is Challenging Yet Rewarding

Many district leaders can attest to the tremendous challenges associated with establishing outstanding schools that generate excellent learning outcomes for all student groups. The political battles of the past decade (often centered upon issues that had little to do with improving student learning outcomes) have only increased the challenges. Table 8.1 describes some of the challenges that are most central to districts' capacity to improve learning results for all student groups.

Chenoweth (2021) asserted clearly and directly, "We can't learn from what we don't know about" (p. 147). Conversations among educators or educational leaders rarely focus on schools where all demographic groups excel. Over time, NCUST has coached leaders of schools with dismal records of student success who wish to improve these circumstances. These leaders appear to have no knowledge of nearby schools serving the same student populations with similar economic and social challenges where twice as many students achieved high rates of success across multiple indicators. There are likely many schools and districts where leaders believe mediocre academic outcomes for students of color, students from low-income homes, and students from other underrepresented groups are as good as can be expected, considering all the factors that impede progress. If leaders believe current learning outcomes are as good as can be reasonably expected, they are not likely to scrutinize their practices to identify improvement opportunities. Likewise, they are not likely to establish ambitious improvement goals or to hold themselves accountable for making progress toward such goals. If leaders do not know the schools described in this book exist, or that others like them exist in their state or in their city, they are not likely to feel any urgency to ensure their schools achieve similar outcomes. If district leaders do not believe academic success for all demographic groups is possible, they will not lead anyone else to believe such success is possible.

Thankfully, many school and district leaders fervently believe their students can achieve outstanding educational outcomes. They know amazing schools that generate increasingly great outcomes for every demographic group they serve. They are convinced that real schools have legitimately achieved outstanding learning results in ways that will ultimately improve the lives of all groups of students. However, if these leaders do not know which gears to turn in order to generate great outcomes in their schools, they will not know how to promote similar successes in their own schools and districts. Many district leaders perish in the gap between what they know is possible and what they know they themselves can influence, especially concerning schools that serve students who traditionally have not been served well.

How many superintendents or district administrators who supervise principals have spent time in an exemplary school observing instruction, observing teacher collaboration, or interviewing teachers and principals? How many district leaders have spent time learning how schools that achieve exemplary results for all students strengthened leadership teams; built positive transformational cultures; enhanced curricular rigor; improved the effectiveness of initial instruction, solidified efforts to monitor, confirm, and enhance learning; and intensified the quality of intervention and enrichment? If district leaders do not realize great learning outcomes are attainable for the students they serve, and if they do not know how to influence the attainment of great learning outcomes for their students, the status quo is not likely to change.

On the other hand, districts such as Brownsville ISD and Garden Grove USD demonstrate the power of district leaders who believe it can be done and who learn how to help schools get it done. One of the assistant superintendents in Brownsville explained how he helps ensure that leaders throughout the system understand how they can influence better learning outcomes. He explained:

> As an assistant superintendent, I make sure we have principals' meetings, cluster meetings, and target meetings. In my cluster meetings, I always bring the bilingual teachers. I bring in other principals to witness what's happening in early childhood education. We just had our cluster meeting a month ago, and all the principals came and visited every classroom. I showed them what a classroom should look like if it's focused on children. And every principal is allowed to take pictures and get artifacts to take back to share with their schools.

Not only can district leaders help school leaders focus attention on the issues that matter most to improve learning outcomes for all students, but wise district leaders can also help minimize the time and energy school leaders spend on issues that are less important. Honig (2012) explained that central office leaders assume a brokering role that links resources to support principals and shield principals from tasks unrelated to improving teaching and learning. District leaders can accelerate improved learning outcomes at all their schools when they believe their schools can generate excellent academic outcomes for all groups of students and when they understand what knowledge, support, and experiences principals and other school leadership team members need in order to improve learning outcomes.

Table 8.1 Challenges and Rewards of District Leadership Support

| Issue | The Challenges | The Rewards |
|---|---|---|
| **Focusing direction in ways that emphasize the overarching purpose of improvement efforts.** | First, district leaders must be convinced that substantially improved academic outcomes and life opportunities are possible for all their students. If district leaders are not convinced, they are unlikely to convince a critical mass of stakeholders. Even when district leaders believe success for all students is possible, leaders can easily cause stakeholders to disengage if they underemphasize the moral imperative and overemphasize compliance with district mandates. | When district leaders help school leaders know that the overarching goal is to help schools generate great outcomes for students, it is much easier for principals and school leadership teams to generate the support necessary from all stakeholders. |
| **Modeling, nurturing, and supporting the development of collaborative cultures.** | In many school districts, structures do not provide the time, resources, or support necessary to build strong collaborative cultures. Even if the structures existed, in many districts, there is not sufficient trust among various stakeholder groups to ensure that collaboration will be fruitful. | When leaders demonstrate their belief that success for all groups of students is not likely to be achieved without rich, meaningful collaboration from all stakeholders, they accelerate the likelihood of district-wide constructive movement. |

(Continued)

Table 8.1 (Continued)

| Issue | The Challenges | The Rewards |
|---|---|---|
| **Supporting change by helping schools measure the movement of the six gears.** | If district leaders do not know what needs to change (the six gears) to maximize the likelihood of great student learning outcomes, they are not likely to be able to help school leadership teams identify measures to gauge improvement related to each gear. Just as importantly, as soon as district leaders start to use measures of improvement in ways that school personnel see as punitive, efforts to improve are likely to be supplanted by efforts to minimally comply. | When district leaders help school leadership teams develop and use measures of improvement in ways that help everyone accelerate movement of the six gears, greater improvement is likely to be achieved and all student groups are likely to benefit. |
| **Nurturing a culture of continuous improvement.** | If district leaders don't understand the changes necessary to improve learning results for all students, they are unlikely to know how to support leadership teams in making the necessary changes. As well, they are unlikely to know how to celebrate important progress that is likely to precede important gains in outcomes. | When district leaders establish and sustain a culture of continuous improvement, the district is much more likely to be able to support schools in improving outcomes for all student groups. |

# District Leadership That Supports School Leadership Teams: What It Is and What It Isn't

## ⊗ What It Isn't: Dictating Change District-Wide

In their sincere desire to support meaningful improvements for students, some well-intentioned district leaders rush to dictate a series of changes related to school culture, curriculum, and instruction. Often, these dictates don't achieve the desired impact in any meaningful way. At times, the district-level mandates work to generate small improvements at some schools; however, rarely are those gains substantial and rarely are they sustained. Often, this lack of impact is due to key stakeholders (e.g., teachers, principals, support staff, parents, students) perceiving the mandates as bureaucratic requirements. If stakeholders don't understand and appreciate the spirit behind district initiatives and if they don't believe district leaders value their perspectives sufficiently to consult with them and engage them in developing solutions, they may rebel or provide only token compliance.

## ✓ What It Is: Inspiring Change District-Wide

In districts that generate broad, sustained efforts to improve learning outcomes for all demographic groups of students, leaders inspire stakeholders by helping everyone believe in their collective ability to improve students' lives. Leaders are able to enlist the energy, talent, and commitment of stakeholders by helping stakeholders know that the district wants what they want for all the district's students. Stakeholders feel valued and respected, yet they also feel challenged to do their best to contribute to comprehensive efforts to improve learning outcomes for all the students they serve.

## ⊗ What It Isn't: Reinforcing Silos

In many school districts, schools operate as if they are disconnected and unrelated to the other schools in the district. Similarly, classrooms operate as if they are disconnected and unrelated to other classrooms down the hall. Consistencies across schools or across classrooms come from mandates associated with state or district policies (e.g., federal programs, attendance monitoring, state testing) or procedural issues that generally convenience district programs (e.g., transportation, food services, technology, textbook adoptions). The silo approach facilitates compliance, but it does little to support improved learning outcomes.

## ✓ What It Is: Building and Reinforcing Collaborative Structures

In districts with multiple NCUST award-winning schools, district leaders promote collaboration at every level. These district leaders assume the best solutions are developed when committed stakeholders support each other in understanding problems of practice, identifying options for addressing those problems, testing those options, measuring their impact, adopting the best ones, and refining the adopted options over time. When situations require top-down solutions, district leaders help stakeholders know why, and they still facilitate collaboration to identify the best ways to implement the solution and yield good results for students.

## ✗ What It Isn't: Expecting Outstanding Results Immediately

In some districts, leaders act as if anyone who is not generating outstanding results is either incompetent or insubordinate. Many stakeholders (e.g., principals, teachers, support staff) become demoralized when they have worked diligently to create foundations for substantially improved learning outcomes; however, they are treated as failures because improved learning results are not yet visible. In such districts, the best employees often find ways to leave and acquire employment in places that recognize and appreciate their efforts. It is interesting to note that many principals of NCUST award-winning schools had prior experience as principals in a different district or as principals under a different area superintendent. Could those principals have achieved outstanding results in their prior assignments if their district leaders had been more supportive of their ideas?

## ✅ What It Is: Creating a Culture of Continuous Improvement

In districts with multiple NCUST award-winning schools, leaders create a culture of continuous improvement by identifying the important elements that are likely to influence improved learning outcomes for all students (i.e., the six gears), working with stakeholders to assess the current status of those elements at each school, and then generating clear strategies to assess/measure improvement of the elements. District leaders support principals and their school leadership teams in prioritizing a few critical concerns at a time. Then, district emphasis is placed on supporting schools in making the few, critical improvements. As, improvements are made, district leaders help school leaders examine leading indicators (early signs) of improvements in learning outcomes. School leaders feel supported in ways that increase the likelihood their schools will successfully improve learning outcomes.

# Tips for District Leaders

*How District Leaders Can Support School Leadership Teams in Advancing the Six Gears (These Tips are Organized to Address Each of the Six Gears, as Presented in This Book)*

### How District Leaders Can Help Schools Establish Effective Leadership Teams

- District leaders should help all stakeholders understand the reason the district is investing in effective leadership teams at each school. The explanation should emphasize the district's commitment to ensuring that all students (and all demographic groups of students) achieve outstanding learning results that will lead them to success at school and success in life. The explanation should also emphasize the district's belief that schools are most likely to generate outstanding learning results for all students if leadership teams work collaboratively with principals, with each other, and with all stakeholder groups to improve the critical elements (i.e., the six gears) that drive success for all student groups.

- District leaders should ensure that all schools have resources to support time for school leadership teams to convene, work with each other, and work with their constituent groups.
- District leaders should model the use of respectful, professional, and inclusive communication processes. School leadership teams should learn that they are expected to use similar processes as they create environments where all students and stakeholder groups feel heard, valued, and connected to efforts to improve learning outcomes. As district leaders model communication efforts that build trust, strengthen relationships, and promote collaborative efforts, they will maximize the likelihood that school leadership teams emulate such communication efforts.
- District leaders should model transparent decision-making, clearly articulate the rationale behind decisions, and help stakeholders understand how decisions support the district's commitment to all students' success.
- District leaders should scrutinize their policies, procedures, and practices related to the hiring of principals and other school administrators. If hiring practices do not prioritize the importance of selecting school leaders who are excellent collaborators, the district may be inadvertently diminishing its chances of having effective school leadership teams.
- District leaders should also scrutinize their policies, procedures, and practices related to the hiring of teachers and other support personnel. If hiring practices do not prioritize the importance of selecting educators who are committed to working with, supporting, and learning from their colleagues, the district may be inadvertently diminishing its chances of having effective school leadership teams.
- District leaders should dedicate professional learning time to ensure that school leadership team members understand how their work must ultimately influence the movement of the six gears described in this book and do so in ways that will advance learning outcomes for all groups of students.
- District leaders should regularly articulate their expectation that school leadership teams will work in ways that build a school-wide belief that the whole school team (teachers, administrators, support staff,

families, community entities, and students) has the capacity to generate outstanding learning outcomes for all groups of students. District leaders should strive to ensure that school leadership team members understand their critical role in building a sense of collective efficacy throughout their school.

- District leaders should work with school leadership teams to develop measures that teams can use to continuously monitor their effectiveness, as they work to advance all six of the gears that drive learning outcomes for all student groups.

## How District Leaders Can Help Schools Build Positive Transformational Cultures

- District leaders should prioritize the development of district policies, procedures, and practices that maximize everyone's physical and emotional safety. With strong district-level policies, procedures, and practices, it should be easier for each school leadership team to ensure implementation and adaptation in ways that increase the likelihood that all students will be eager to come to school and learn, all parents will be eager to work with school personnel to advance the success of their children, and all school personnel will be eager to come to work with a team they perceive is making a powerful difference in the lives of children.

- District leaders should encourage every school leadership team to examine quantitative and qualitative data that might indicate that some groups of children feel less welcome, less valued, less respected, or less capable at school. District leaders should challenge leadership teams to ensure every child (regardless of race/ethnicity, gender, family income, housing status, language background, age, behavior record, academic record, disability status, or any other factor) concludes that their school has been designed to guarantee their success in school and their success in life.

- District leaders should encourage every school leadership team to strive to make every school employee believe they were hired because they were perceived to have knowledge, skills, and dispositions that could help the school achieve outstanding learning results for all students.

- District leaders should provide professional learning opportunities within which school leadership teams learn how to establish and nurture positive transformational cultures for school personnel, families, and students.

## How District Leaders Can Help Schools Strengthen Rigorous Curricula

- District leaders should ensure that school leadership teams have the time, resources, and expert support they need to generate consensus about the essential concepts and skills all students should learn.

- District leaders should support opportunities for school leadership teams to share and learn from each other about the essential concepts and skills they expect all students to learn. In particular, district leaders should support vertical collaboration (e.g., elementary schools, middle schools, and high schools) so that students are likely to experience a high likelihood of success as they transition from one level to the next.

- District leaders should encourage school leadership teams to embrace high expectations for all students. At the same time, district leaders should expect school leadership teams to think deliberately about what supports teachers will need, and what supports students will need, to meet the high expectations.

## How District Leaders Can Help Schools Strengthen Effective Initial Instruction

- District leaders should encourage opportunities for school leadership team members to see many examples of effective initial instruction. School leadership team members should have opportunities to see excellent instructional practices, ask questions about the practices, learn about the nuances that help the practice make a difference (especially for student groups that historically have been underserved), and plan strategies for helping each other implement the practices well.

- District leaders should encourage school leadership teams to use practices, such as affirming learning walks (Ross, Lamb, & Johnson, 2023), to engage their colleagues in learning about effective initial instruction practices and then visiting each other to identify and describe positive examples of the practices in their classrooms. The affirming learning walks should build enthusiasm about the teams' collective efforts to learn from each other and support each other in implementing powerful initial instruction practices.

- District leaders should encourage principals and school leadership teams to focus improvement efforts over an extended period of time on a small number of powerful instructional practices. District leaders should encourage schools to develop a few specific "signature practices" that all students will experience and benefit from in every classroom throughout the school. District leaders should encourage leadership teams to determine non-punitive ways to identify the school's progress in developing excellent implementation so that the practice becomes a valued feature of the school.

- District leaders should encourage collaboration between schools that choose to focus on the same or similar "signature practice." This school-to-school collaboration could help educators learn how their colleagues at a different school implement and refine important instructional practices.

- District leaders should find small and large ways to acknowledge the progress school teams make in improving implementation of "signature practices." In acknowledging improvement efforts, district leaders should emphasize the positive impact on learning results for students.

- Even in times of reduced resources, district leaders should prioritize school-based time and resources to support instructional improvement efforts. Effective collaboration fuels improvement. The absence of time and support for effective collaboration will minimize the impact of all other investments (e.g., new curricula, new technology, increased instructional minutes).

## How District Leaders Can Help Schools Strengthen Efforts to Monitor, Confirm, and Enhance Learning

- District leaders should be cautious about the use of any district assessment that cannot easily be used by school personnel to monitor, confirm, and enhance student learning. Instead, district leaders should ensure that any district-wide assessment will generate immediate data that will allow principals and school leadership teams to understand specifically which important concepts and skills students mastered and which students are yet to master. The best assessments are those that will help leadership teams enhance learning by showing teachers, "Here's what we need to teach next week to lead our students to a deep understanding of this concept."

- District leaders should organize professional learning experiences that help school leadership teams know how to develop short, precise formative assessments that help teachers know what students understand, what they don't yet understand, and what might be interfering with student understanding. Professional learning should support leadership teams in promoting rigorous formative assessments that provide teachers an accurate picture of how students understand challenging academic concepts. As well, professional learning experiences should be designed to build the capacity of school leadership teams to support their colleagues in using formative assessments to determine appropriate next steps for improving instruction and enhancing learning.

- District leaders should encourage collaboration among school leadership teams so teams can learn from each other's best practices for communicating learning progress to students and families. District leaders should encourage transparency, promote the use of effective tools (including the use of technology to communicate learning progress), and foster the meaningful engagement of students and families so student-learning progress inspires even greater effort and progress.

## How District Leaders Can Help Schools Improve Intervention and Enrichment

- District leaders should work with school leadership teams to design professional learning opportunities that help educators understand the limitations of traditional practices concerning intervention and enrichment. As well, professional learning opportunities should help leadership teams promote alternatives to traditional practices, such as immediate, laser-focused intervention (instead of delayed and generic intervention) and enrichment for all (instead of enrichment experiences exclusively for students who experienced early learning success).

- District leaders should promote collaboration among school leadership teams that highlights the best practices used to pinpoint students' misconceptions and plan intervention that is laser focused on eliminating those misconceptions.

- District leaders should promote collaboration among school leadership teams that highlights the best practices used to provide all students excellent enrichment opportunities that engage students in applying the concepts and skills they are learning to real-life situations relevant to their lives, their communities, and their interests. Collaboration should be structured in ways that encourage teams to learn from and use each other's best practices for teaching challenging concepts and skills in ways students perceive as relevant and engaging.

## References

Bryk, A. S., Gomez, L. M., Grunow, A., & LeMahieu, P. G. (2015). *Learning to improve: How America's schools can get better at getting better.* Cambridge, MA: Harvard Education Press.

Chenoweth, K. (2021). *Districts that succeed: Breaking the correlation between race, poverty, and achievement.* Cambridge, MA: Harvard Education Press.

Fullan, M., & Quinn, J. (2016). *Coherence: The right drivers in action for schools, districts, and systems.* Thousand Oaks, CA: Corwin.

Honig, M. I. (2012). District central office leadership as teaching: How central office administrators support principals' development as instructional leaders. *Educational Administration Quarterly, 48*(4), 733–774.

Johnson, J. F., Uline, C. L., & Perez, L. G. (2017). *Leadership in America's best urban schools.* New York: Routledge and Taylor & Francis Group.

Knudson, J. (2013). *You'll never be better than your teachers: The Garden Grove approach to human capital development* (California Collaborative on District Reform). Washington, DC: American Institutes for Research.

Rorrer, A. K., Skrla, L., & Scheurich, J. J. (2008). Districts as institutional actors in educational reform. *Educational Administration Quarterly, 44*(3), 307–358. doi: 10.1177/0013161X08318962

Ross, D. L., Lamb, L. L., & Johnson, J. F. (2023). Using affirming learning walks to build capacity. *Journal of School Administration Research and Development, 8*(1), 47–54.

Tschannen-Moran, M. (2014). *Trust matters: Leadership in successful schools* (2nd ed.). San Francisco, CA: Jossey-Bass.

WestEd. (2019). *We shake hands at the door: The power of relationships in schools.* Retrieved from https://wested2024.s3.us-west-1.amazonaws.com/wp-content/uploads/2024/07/11170044/resource-we-shake-hands-at-the-door-how-a-focus-on-relationships-is-driving-improvement-in-chula-vista.pdf

# Conclusion

We, the authors of this book, have been especially fortunate to have enjoyed many amazing opportunities to observe, study, and learn from talented educators, inspiring leaders, brilliant change agents, and fantastic human beings who have dedicated their professional lives to improving the trajectory of students' lives. We hope these pages showcase their wisdom, common sense, people skills, tenacity, teamwork, love of children, and love of learning. Just as importantly, however, we hope we have reflected onto these pages their practical efforts to think systematically about how to improve schools in ways that will improve students' lives.

We hope we have accurately described the substantial challenges you and your colleagues are likely to face as you seek to further transform your school or district to become a place where all students are likely to experience academic successes that will lead to successes throughout their lives. At the same time, we hope we have accurately explained how you, as a committed team of leaders, can work together to ensure you overcome the challenges in ways that will make your school and district a model for others across your state or our nation.

After reading this book, we hope you see more clearly than ever: it can be done! Your school or your district can become a place where all students, regardless of demographic characteristics, can achieve excellent learning outcomes. Mortal educators have changed their schools in ways that are transforming lives! Hopefully, you see specific ways you and your colleagues can build upon your strengths in ways that move your school or district forward.

Perhaps, most importantly, however, we hope that the stories and descriptions of the award-winning schools featured in these pages encourage you and your colleagues to continue growing, learning, and strengthening the elements that drive improved learning outcomes for all student groups. Toward this end, we hope you visit some NCUST award-winning schools or other schools that achieve outstanding results for all demographic groups of students. The full list of award-winning schools is available at https://ncust.com/previous-americas-best-urban-schools-award-winners/. We would love to see you at an NCUST America's Best Schools Virtual Symposium where we provide educators a multitude of rich opportunities to engage with teachers and leaders from America's Best Schools, learn more about how they grappled with problems similar to the challenges you face at your school, and learn how they continue to struggle with frustrating issues (even though they have achieved national recognition for their successes).

Ultimately, we hope your school or multiple schools in your district come to meet NCUST award criteria. The criteria can be found at https://ncust.com/americas-best-urban-schools-award-eligibility-criteria/. Whether your school appears to be far away or remarkably close to qualifying, we hope the criteria inspire your continued growth and improvement. Honestly, NCUST's recognition is a small award. The big award is the knowledge that you and your colleagues have made a powerful difference in the lives of the students you've had the honor to serve.

For Product Safety Concerns and Information please contact our EU
representative GPSR@taylorandfrancis.com
Taylor & Francis Verlag GmbH, Kaufingerstraße 24, 80331 München, Germany

www.ingramcontent.com/pod-product-compliance
Lightning Source LLC
Chambersburg PA
CBHW062224300426

44115CB00012BA/2213